Pirates and Piracy

Pirates and Piracy

David Reinhardt

Grange
BOOKS

This edition first published in 1997 for Grange Books
An imprint of Grange Books Plc
The Grange
Grange Yard
London SE1 3AG

This edition by arrangement W. S. Konecky Associates

ISBN: 1-84013-066-0

Book design by STUDIO 31, INC.

Printed in the U.S.A.

Dedicated to
the memory of my father

JOHN J. REINHARDT, JR.

Contents

A Brief History of Piracy

Piracy in the Ancient World

Piracy is an ancient profession. In the Mediterranean piracy flourished as an adjunct to the growth of maritime commerce. The Hellenic world was plagued with pirates, who not only boarded vessels at sea but would also organize raids on land. In his account of the Peloponnesian Wars, Thucydides observes that Minos, king of Crete was the first to raise a navy, doing so in large measure to suppress the piracy that had become a drain on his treasury. He also notes an ambivalence in the way piracy was viewed, an ambivalence that has persisted to the present day. For although pirates were rightly hated and feared, the freedom of their way of life was attractive to many, even the well-born. Here is the first suggestion of what would become a commonplace in pirate literature and legend: the noble hero whose sense of adventure takes him to the high seas. A charming later example of this is to be found in Gilbert & Sullivan's operetta *The Pirates of Penzance*, where we learn at the denouement that the pirates are "all noblemen who have gone wrong."

Thucydides paints a detailed picture of how pirates plied their trade in the Hellenic world:

> For in these early times as communication by sea became easier, so piracy became a common profession both among the Hellenes and among the barbarians who lived on the coast and the islands. The leading pirates were powerful men, acting both out of self-interest and in order to support the weak among their own people. They would descend upon cities which were unprotected by walls and

OPPOSITE — *An Attack on a Galleon*. Howard Pyle.

Attic vase showing Greek warship (Louvre, Art Resource, N.Y.)

indeed consisted only of scattered settlements; and by plundering such places they would gain most of their livelihood. At this time such a profession, so far from being regarded as disgraceful, was considered quite honorable. It is an attitude that can be illustrated even today by some of the inhabitants of the mainland among whom successful piracy is regarded as something to be proud of; and in the old poets, too, we find that the regular question always asked of those who arrive by sea is "Are you pirates?" It is never assumed either that those who were so questioned would shrink from admitting the fact, or that those who were interested in finding out the fact would reproach them with it.

The Roman republic also had to contend with piracy. During the second century B.C. Rome destroyed the naval power of Rhodes, which until that time had acted as a restraining influence on the worst depredations of marauding pirate bands. In the fleet's absence piracy flourished from its base in Cilicia on the coast of Asia Minor. At the end of the century, under Marcus Antonius the Romans declared war on the pirates. Notwithstanding, their strength increased over the next forty years until they were in virtual control of the Mediterranean. Ports in Italy were closed; the pirates even raided Rome's home port of Ostia, where according to Cicero, "almost before Rome's eyes the consul's fleet was captured and destroyed."

Rome was by this time dependent on produce from its colonies to feed its growing population. Threatened with the prospect of famine and financial ruin, the senate, with the passage of the Gabinian law, granted Pompey unprecedented powers to eliminate this menace. Pompey succeeded brilliantly and swept the sea clean of pirates within three months. His victories signaled an end to piracy as a significant problem in the Roman world.

During their heyday pirates lived in luxury and attracted many men of noble birth. Plutarch in his *Life of Pompey* provides a look at their manner of life:

Single-masted Greek merchantman (Museum of Science, Milan, Art Resource, N.Y.).

Lateen-rigged Roman merchant vessel (Alinari/Art Resource, N.Y.)

And now even men of great wealth, of noble birth, of outstanding reputation for good sense, embarked on ... these freebooting adventures as if this occupation brought honor and distinction ... The envy they aroused and their ostentation was even more irksome than the dread they caused. Their ships had gilded flag masts at the stern, purple hangings, and silvered oars, as if they reveled and gloried in their evildoing. There was music and dancing and carousal on every shore.

The pirates' fortunes recovered as the Roman Empire sickened; but with the fall of Rome trade declined sharply. In its aftermath pirates confined themselves to the richer trading routes of the eastern Mediterranean and North Africa. And although throughout the Middle Ages piracy was common practice it was not until the discovery of the New World and its vast stores of riches that pirates once again became masters of the sea.

The Golden Age
of Piracy

The main focus of this book is on the Caribbean in the late seventeenth and early eighteenth centuries. This particular era witnessed the greatest flourishing of piracy and produced some of its most memorable characters. For this reason it has been dubbed the golden age of piracy. Never before and never since has there been such a proliferation of the trade both in numbers of practitioners and in the scope of their operations.

This period could with equal justice be named the golden age of sail. Starting in the middle of the fifteenth century, as with many other fields of human endeavor, technological innovations led to significant developments in nautical science. Progress in ship design was especially important. Three-masted carracks with square driving sails on the main and foremasts began to replace older lateen-rigged vessels — that is single-masted ships propelled by a triangular sail set at a 45 degree angle to the yard. These improvements made longer voyages possible. The *Santa Maria*, Columbus's flagship, was a three-masted carrack.

A number of historical conditions combined with technological developments to foster the perfect environment for the rapid growth and success of piracy in the Caribbean during this period. But behind them all was one simple ruling factor: money. On his way to opening up a new, faster route to the wealth of east Asia, Columbus stumbled upon a continent that hitherto had been completely unknown in Europe. His inadvertent discovery marks the beginning of the modern era. It changed the

Fifteenth century single-masted merchant ship. From stained glass window commissioned by Jacques Le Coeur (Hôtel Jacques Le Coeur, Bourges, Giraudon/ Art Resource, N.Y.).

Print showing the cartographer Petrus Plancius using an astrolabe. Three-masted ship is lateen rigged on the main and mizzen with a square-rigged sail on the foremast and sprit sail under the bowsprit. By Galle after Stradanus (Netherlands Historic Maritime Museum, Amsterdam).

economic structure of the European continent and would lead to the age of colonial empires and European dominance on the world stage. Following the routes charted by Columbus, the Spanish Crown set out upon the systematic exploration, colonization, and exploitation of the New World.

Europe was soon to become very rich. A vast, seemingly inexhaustible amount of gold, silver, and jewels was now making its way by sea into the coffers of the Spanish monarchy. Shipbuilding and armaments were only the first industries to be affected in what was to become a burst of economic activity. This in turn would lead to a flourishing merchant class accompanied by modernization of the banking industry. The plunder from the New World made the Spanish court the envy of Europe and sparked its imperial aspirations.

French buccaneer Pierre François boarding the *Vice-Admiral,* a Spanish man-of-war. His exploits are detailed in Esquemelin's *Buccaneers of America.* Artist unknown (Hulton Getty Picture Collection, London).

News of vast wealth in the Americas spread from Spain throughout Europe. In 1522 a French corsair, Jean Fleury, captured the Spanish caravel bearing part of Montezuma's treasure sent by Hernán Cortés. The treasure was unloaded in Dieppe to the astonishment of the bystanders. It was the first glimpse outside of Spain and Portugal of the waiting riches in the New World. In the same year François I, the king of France, was heard to express a desire to see the clause in Adam's will that divided up the world between Portugal and Spain.

The English began raiding Spanish merchant vessels when they were prohibited from trading with Spanish ports. To protect its interests, Spain erected forts manned with garrisons at ports and other strategic points in its colonial empire.

Richard Halkyut in his justly famous work, *Principle Navigations, Voyages, Traffiques and Discoveries of the English Nation* (1589), eloquently describes the position the English and French faced with Iberian dominance of the New World: "Seeing that the wealth of the Spaniards & Portuguese, by the discovery of new trades and countries was marvelously increased, supposing the same to be a course and a mean for them also

Portrait of Hernán Cortés. Artist unknown (Muséo de Santa Cruz, Toledo, Spain).

to obtain the like, they therefore resolved upon a new and a strange navigation."

It was inevitable that France and Britain would challenge Spain's claims to the riches of the new continent. Their policy of harassing Spanish shipping and launching their own expeditions to search for a northern passage to the Orient helped set the stage over which the black flag of piracy would be raised.

Much has been written about the Spanish Main. Technically, the Spanish Main referred to the Caribbean coasts of present-day Panama, Colombia, and western Venezuela. This curious name dates from the earliest sixteenth century, when the first explorers ventured beyond the Caribbean isles in search of what they believed to be the nearby Asian continent. By coincidence, the first large land mass they charted contiguously proved to be that of northern South America, which the Spaniards dubbed Tierra Firma — the Mainland. Even after further explorations revealed this to be but a portion of a vast new continent, it remained customary to refer to this particular stretch of coastline by its original name. From Spanish the expression passed into English, soon being shortened to the "Spanish Main" and occasionally misapplied to the waters lying off that coast, rather than the territory itself.

The most successful of the early Spanish conquistadors, Hernán Cortés fought his way onto the continent, and with a combination of guile and brute force overthrew the vast Aztec empire and established the Spanish kingdom of Mexico. From this base other expeditions were launched, including those of Francisco Pizarro, who conquered the Incan kingdom in Peru and laid claim to vast deposits of silver. Ships carrying the spoils of the great Pre-Columbian empires back to Spain used the islands of the Caribbean as staging points. It was here that the other continental powers, France, Holland, and England, began to chip away at Spain's hegemony, establishing settlements on small islands close by Spanish shipping lanes. The conditions were ideal for piracy and privateering.

In 1654 Oliver Cromwell attempted to gain a foothold in the Caribbean for England. He had his sights set on Santo Domingo, the Spanish capital of Hispaniola. When the attack was repulsed, the expeditionary force retreated to Jamaica, beginning a presence that has lasted until the present day. It is possible that the renowned pirate Henry Morgan earned his stripes on this expedition. Early on the French arrived in Hispaniola. Roving bands of lawless French hunters had settled the wilder parts of the island and naturally came into conflict with the Spanish authorities. It was from these hunters' practice of smoking meat in an oven called a *boucan* that the term buccaneer derives.

The Spanish inhabitants of the region resisted any encroachments on territory they considered theirs by right. Hatreds that were playing out on the Continent were mirrored in the Caribbean. Pirates and privateers flourished in this stormy political climate. Vast wealth was there for the

"The Buccaneer Was a Picturesque Fellow." Howard Pyle.

taking, and patriotic sentiment could be made to justify the most savage behavior. The struggle for power lasted through the end of the century, despite various peace treaties such as that concluded between England and Spain in 1670. Bitter enmity kept tensions high and contributed to atrocities committed on all sides.

Since no government would officially stand behind the criminal act of piracy, even against a dreaded enemy, an extremely useful innovation was the "letters of marque." These letters were official sanctions to harass, capture, and plunder the merchant vessels of a hostile nation. They created an auxiliary navy with the sole and terribly important purpose of damaging the enemy nation's war efforts by cutting into its trade and thus its ability to raise and supply armies and navies. One clear advantage of sailing under letters of marque was that should the crew be captured they were regarded as combatants rather than pirates and thus were not subject to the penalty of hanging.

The major maritime powers liberally granted letters of marque. The earliest known grant in England was made by Henry IV in the early fifteenth century to two Bristol vessels. The most successful of English privateers, Francis Drake, became a national hero for his attacks on Spanish ships and colonies and was knighted by Queen Elizabeth. In France the exploits of privateers such as Jean Bart and Jacques Crassard, who attacked English shipping in the North Sea and the Channel, became the stuff of legend. A little later on American privateers established themselves as a formidable presence. In the first half of the eighteenth century hundreds of privateers sailed from colonial ports. The American privateer fleet during the Revolutionary War effectively blocked the British from the ports that remained under their control.

There were definite incentives for private ship owners to engage in privateering. During times of hostilities, when normal trade was often disrupted, they could make use of their idle ships to capture enemy cargoes. The ship owners were expected to declare their prizes but were allowed to keep a percentage of the value of the captured goods and money.

Of course, there was a fine line between privateering and piracy, and its definition usually depended on which side you were on in a dispute. Privateering turned out to be as much a curse as a blessing for the governments of Europe. As history has repeatedly proven, the use of mercenary forces carries a heavy price. While the privateers proved tremendously helpful during time of war, they were a problem once peace was declared and the harbors were filled with heavily armed private ships. Manned by crews facing the serious prospect of unemployment, the erstwhile privateers knew that plundering merchant vessels provided a good living and had become skilled in the practice.

Different sovereigns had their own ideas about both privateering and piracy. While most admitted, privately if not publicly, that privateering

Portrait of Sir Francis Drake. Artist unknown (National Portrait Gallery, London).

Capture of H.B.M. Frigate *Macedonian* by U.S. Frigate *United States* during the War of 1812. Thomas Chambers (National Museum of American Art/ Art Resource, N.Y.)

was a necessary if not wholly scrupulous practice, they held various views on piracy. Most saw it as a disruption of normal trade and therefore a hindrance to be dealt with as one might deal with highwaymen or other robbers and thieves. There were monarchs who took a decidedly tough tack with piracy. James I observed that piracy had become "too deeply rooted among" his English subjects. His predecessor, Elizabeth I, lent aid and encouragement to privateers. The English had become identified as a nation of pirates. This image persisted well beyond the reign of James I, has been sustained in literature, and has now become fixed in the popular mind. In England, as in the ancient world, there was an ambivalent attitude toward piracy. Pirates were in turn lauded and despised. It was not until the beginning of the eighteenth century, as the island found itself strangled by the unchecked growth of piracy, that the crown finally set out to eradicate this infection.

Piracy was not the chief national or international problem faced by England during the reign of the Stuarts, but as Sir John Digby advised James I, it was like "a thorn in the foot — painful and crippling — hurtful enough to compel one to seek a remedy." Sometimes naval force was employed while at other times diplomacy or appeasement was favored. It is fair to state that the ebb and flow of English piracy was directly affect-

Privateer Ship *Grand Turk*. One of the most successful American ships during the war of 1812. It captured 39 British ships in the course of its career (Peabody Essex Museum, Salem Mass.).

ed by the political events on the Continent and England's relations with the continental powers.

Since England spent a great deal of the late seventeenth and early eighteenth centuries in and out of war with France and Spain, there was a steady increase in the number of English pirates and privateers. These conflicts also led to the expansion of the Royal Navy and merchant shipping. Both provided rich pools of discontented labor, who, when faced with the prospect of unemployment, were more than happy to sign the articles for a pirate ship and enter what promised to be a free and exceedingly well-remunerated career.

Political and economic forces in Europe were at work forging a new ideology, that of the modern state. But its emergence seemed to require continual warfare. The Dutch-Anglo Wars were in effect a series of protracted skirmishes, but they lasted throughout much of the middle of the century. Meanwhile France under Louis XIV was becoming as the pre-eminent continental power. His rivalry with Spain led to attacks on the

OVERLEAF — Map of the Caribbean. From William Russell, *The History of America,* 1778.

THE
WEST INDIES,
and
GULF of MEXICO,
from the latest Discoveries
and
Best Observations.

ATLANTIC

Tropic of Cancer

OCEAN

CAYOS OR BAHAMA ISLANDS

Eucayos
the Hole in the Rock
Harbour I.
Cigateo or
Alebaster I.
Eleuthera
Guanahana or
Cat Island.
The First Land in
America discov.d by
Columbus 1492.
Watling
Exuma
Long
Isle
Rum Key
Samana or
Crooked I.
Atwoods Key
Mayaguana or Mogane
Fortune I.
Flat I.
Acklins Key
Mira porvos
Caycos
French Key
North Key
Turks I.
Abreojo by the French
le Mouchoir quarre
Vigia
Cayos de Plata
or Silver Keys

CARIBBE

CUBA
WINDWARD
LE CAP
Old Cape Francois
S. Jago
HISPANIOLA OR St. DOMINGO
SAN DOMINGO
PORTO RICO
VIRGIN Isles
St. Croix Da.

ANTILLES

St. Christopher F.
Barbuda E.
ANTIGUA E.
GUADALOUPE F.
Marie Galante E.
Dominica E.

LEEWARD Is.

Aves I.

CARIBBEAN SEA.

MARTINICO F.
St. Lucia
BARBADOS E.
St. Vincent
Cannaouan I.
GRANADA E.
TABAGO N.

WINDWARD Is.

LITTLE ANTILLES

CURAZAO D.
Aruba D.
Bonair D.
Orchilla
7 Ages
MARGARITA
Testigos
St. Giles Pt.

Rock

CARTHAGENA
Sta. MARTHA
VENEZUELA
Maracaybo
CARACCAS
COMANA
PARIA
TRINIDAD
St. Thomas

TIERRA FIRMA
R. Orinoco

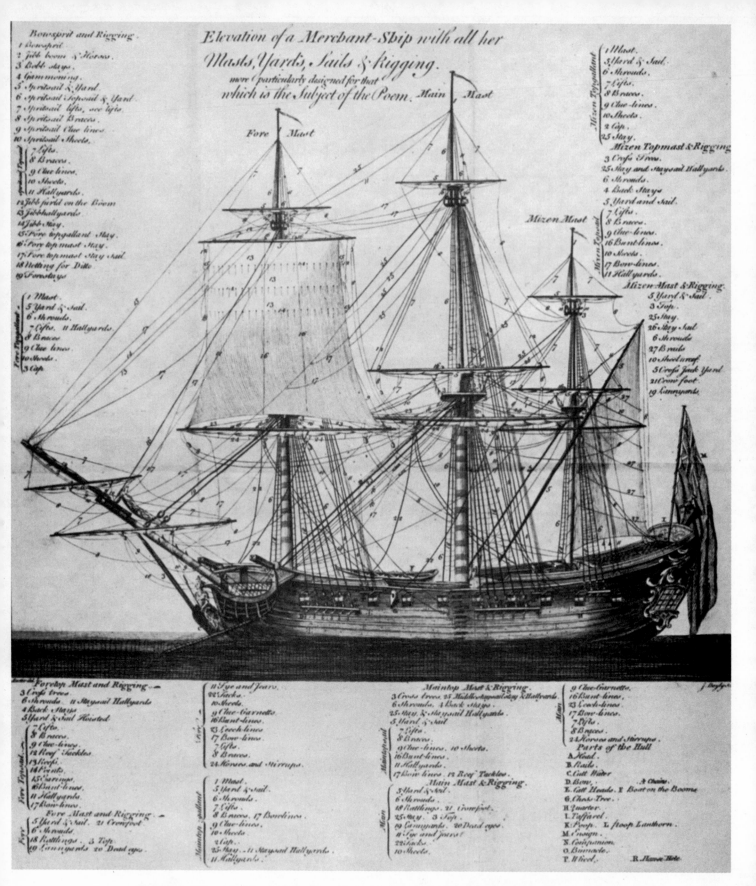

Rigging of a merchant ship. Engraving by an unknown artist for William
Falconer's poem "Shipwreck," 1762.

28

Netherlands, and with the Peace of Nijmegen in 1678, Spain's influence in Northern Europe came to an end. Alarmed at France's growing strength, former enemies, England and Holland, entered into alliance that ultimately checked France's expansionist aims. But it was not until the Treaty of Utrecht in 1713 that a workable equilibrium between the major powers was achieved.

The conflicts between the European powers inevitably spilled over into their colonial possessions. It is fair to say that the Caribbean privateers, who were ostensibly acting in the national interest, often took advantage of the uncertainty of international relations to secure their own. Henry Morgan, for example, launched his raid on Panama while peace was being negotiated between England and Spain. It was for this reason that he was arrested and brought back to England.

Ultimately the success of pirates and privateers was subject to political considerations. As they began to prosper they invited more attention to themselves. Privateers certainly had their uses, but they were generally unreliable and becoming more trouble than they were worth. Violence and brutality were on the rise and commercial interests were seriously threatened. Woodes Rogers, the governor of Nassau, whose success combating piracy was unequaled, began his crusade because pirates were harassing his merchant ships.

The disputes between France and Spain were especially bitter. The French pirate Jean Nau, perhaps the cruelest of all time, vowed to exterminate every Spaniard he came in contact with. Reports of his death were met with large-scale rejoicing in Spanish settlements up and down the Spanish Main.

As the historian, David Marley, notes, "The prolonged war which then ensued, pitting France against Spain and Holland during the remainder of the 1670s, provided ample employment for a whole new generation of mercenaries who continued to mount assaults even after peace had been restored back in Europe by the Treaty of Nijmegen ..."

The havoc wreaked by maritime mercenaries was severe and costly. The next fifty years would witness an explosion of attacks on merchant and naval vessels and the arrival on the scene of the most notorious pirates. Soon names such as Bartholomew Roberts, Henry Every, William Kidd and Blackbeard would strike terror in the hearts of travellers and traders. Whether their reputation for ferocity was truly deserved is an open question. By and large pirates were out for what they could get. And if the black flags and jolly rogers that identified their ships filled their victims with fear and persuaded them to surrender more readily, so much the better. Blackbeard, credited with being one of the fiercest in his trade, seems to have made deliberate use of scare tactics to avoid engagements that would lead to bloodshed.

Eventually the pirates themselves became the victims, of their own success. The renown of the most successful captains inspired many to take to the seas. The most famous pirate of the time, Henry Every, was a kind of celebrity in England, whose adventures were closely followed in the press. The Caribbean was overflowing with pirates, until there was just not enough booty to go around. The careers of some pirates, operating at the end of this period, are rather pathetic. Calico Jack for example had to resort to raiding small fishing boats and stealing livestock just to keep his crew from starving. Perhaps he was second rate pirate, but vast hoards of treasure were no longer easy to come by.

At the same time outside pressures were increasing. By the end of the seventeenth century England had established itself as the dominant naval power. The Crown, which had often turned a blind eye to the maraudings of pirates and privateers, especially when their targets were Spanish and Dutch, began to experience a change of heart. The trial of William Kidd at the turn of the century was a sign of things to come. The colonial governors in North America found themselves forced by landowners and merchants to forgo the profits that they had been raking off the top from pirates working their waters and act to quell activities that were threatening the general prosperity.

As a consequence of these and other factors, the center of pirate activity shifted from the Caribbean to the Indian Ocean. It was there that Bartholomew Roberts captured his richest hauls, and Henry Every almost started an international incident by capturing the richest vessel in the fleet of Aurangzeb, the ruler of India. Pirate activity centered around the island of Madagascar, which soon rivalled New Providence in the Caribbean as a favorite haunt for freebooters.

By 1720 the great age of piracy had ended. Though the Barbary corsairs remained unchecked, their activities were confined to the Mediterranean. The great pirates had either been killed in battle, captured and hanged, or in the exceptional case, as with Every, settled down to enjoy their profits and lead a life of comfortable obscurity. The power of the Royal Navy was now undisputed master of the seas, and maritime commerce had become too important to jeapordize. The new century was to bring enlightenment and revolution. Pirates began to recede into the realm of legend and imagination.

A Pirate's Life

WHY A PIRATE?

Why would someone choose a life of piracy? There certainly seem to be some common denominators in the backgrounds of most pirates. With very few exceptions, such as Bartholomew Roberts, pirates came from poor backgrounds. A life at sea offered a means of survival at a time when thousands of people literally were starving on the streets of the capitals of Europe.

People came to piracy via different routes. Some began as pirates, but they were far more likely to have first seen service in the navy or the merchant marine.

Of course, there were also privateers, but there was a fine line between privateering and piracy. Technically, as long as privateers acted in strict accordance with their commissions, they were deemed to be operating within the law.

Because privateers were already experienced raiders and plunderers, and all too aware of the riches to be had, they easily could turn to piracy. In times of peace the temptation was especially strong, especially in view of the high unemployment rates back in Europe.

Nor is it difficult to understand why many sailors came to piracy through legitimate naval service. The harsh reality of maritime service was described by an eighteenth century mariner who explained the social logic of life at sea to a "green hand:"

Pirate schooner preparing to board a merchantman. Artist unknown (Snark/ Art Resource, N.Y.)

There is no justice or injustice on board ship, my lad. There are only two things: duty and mutiny — mind that. All that you are ordered to do is duty. All that you refuse to do is mutiny.

Many captains ruled their ships along precisely these lines. They were aided in their efforts by the fact that once a ship had sailed beyond the confines of a port it was nearly impossible for anyone or anything to control the captain's actions. The ship was a world unto itself in which the captain had formal powers over the labor process, the dispensing of food, the maintenance of health, and the general social life on board ship. Such formal and informal controls invested the captain with near-dictatorial powers and made the ship the equivalent of a totalitarian state.

One of the main enforcers of the principle of obedience, an essential component of the captain's authority, was the cat-of-nine-tails, the legendary emblem of maritime brutality. The captain's armory might also be well stocked with canes, ropes, belts, sticks, and numerous other objects that could be made to function as weapons.

Cruelty was widespread and passed as the rule rather than the exception. Some blood curdling accounts exist. One such deposition tells of a John Pattison, foremast man on the *Unity,* who, while sailing to the West Indies in 1708, failed to remember a chore. He was seized "by the hair of his head" by Captain Matthew Beesley. The captain then forced his head "under the 2nd gun on the Larboard side" and beat him with "a great Roap...so long and in such a barbarous and cruel manner that . . . Pattison for some time after was scarcely able to lift his head." Beesley, Pattison deposed, "would then have certainly murdered or crippled" him "had not the Gunner or some other persons cryed out Shame on it" and

Flogging was the chief method of enforcing discipline in the merchant fleet and the Royal Navy. Etching by George Cruikshank. From *Old Ship Prints* by E. Keble Chatterton, 1825.

A pirate on the scaffold at Execution Dock. Artist Unknown (National Maritime Museum, London).

thereby "prevented him." On the occasion of other beatings Beesley caused "almost a pinte of Blood" to flow from Pattison's nose.

Some of the beatings given sailors by captains were vicious almost beyond belief. Captain William Newcomin in 1733 beat John Jones with a stone mug and "broke four of his teeth quite out of his head." James Conroy testified in 1707 that his captain, a Mr. Wherry, "catched him fast by the Nose with his left hand and thrust" into his "left Eye and with his right hand struck three Blows on his said thumb and in that manner willfully, designedly and maliciously maimed and put out" his eye.

Cruelties such as these represented a tactic of authority central to maritime discipline — intimidation. Authority at sea was intensely personal, which in turn was the very basis of intimidation. Undoubtedly, the men described previously were used as examples to the rest of the crew. Even Captain Woodes Rogers, later a revered figure, had one seaman "severely whipt before the Whole Company as a Terror to the rest."

It is impossible to know how many sailors were murdered, primarily because the existing records are profoundly incomplete.

Responsibility for the rationing of food was an important part of the captain's near-dictatorial control over the ship. Withholding sustenance from the crew was used as a means of discipline, and was especially important in the merchant navy, since any money saved on this account increased the profitability of the voyage for the owners. Although the captain was enjoined by law "to provide his seamen aboard ship with good food and living conditions," such injunctions were often disregarded.

Another means of punishment was confinement. Seamen were often chained either in a dark hold, or on deck with no protection against inclement weather.

These were the tactics most frequently employed in a system of authority best described as violent, personal and arbitrary. It is little wonder then, that when faced with the chance to "turn pirate" many sailors welcomed the opportunity. After enduring such cruelty, the thought of

Pirates drinking, *Pirate's Own Book*, 1837

35

having a vote in the government of a ship, which was the custom among pirates, must have seemed like a dream come true. So harsh were the conditions of the life of an honest seaman that the possibility of being captured as a pirate and the prospect of hanging offered little deterrence.

ELECTING A CAPTAIN

The captain of a pirate crew had the great aft cabin to himself, but any man on board had the right to enter the cabin at any time, take a drink from the captain's supply of rum, and even swear at him. In fact, these privileges were rarely used, and it was usual for the pirate captain to be treated with a great deal of respect.

When a pirate captain was chosen there was usually some ceremony surrounding his taking "office." After the company had elected him, the quartermaster or another of the men's leaders would make a speech wishing him prosperity and a long and healthy term. He would then be led in a formal procession to the great cabin and requested to have a seat at the head of the table. The quartermaster would join him as representative of the entire ship's company. Unsheathing a sword he would present this to the captain, accompanied by a brief statement to the following effect, "We hereby commission you to lead us. May you bring us and yourself good fortune!"

At the end of the ceremony the hands would fire all guns. The captain would then invite the senior men of the crew to dine with him. The rest of the crew would proceed to get roaring drunk, except for the musicians, who were typically forced men — serving on the ship against their will. They had to remain sober and keep playing until their audience drifted into a deep and soundless oblivion.

"FORCED" MEN AND WALKING THE PLANK

Once a prize had been taken and her cargo seized and inspected the pirates would turn their attention to dealing with the crew. Young men, likely to be strong and good sailors, would be interviewed by the captain or quartermaster, and asked to sign the ship's articles. To be invited to join the crew in this manner was really just a formality. There was not much real choice involved. Even if a man refused, he was usually "forced" to serve, and there was better feeling if he joined his captives voluntarily. The one benefit, and it was a major one, to being "forced"

OPPOSITE — Walking the Plank. Howard Pyle.

was that if the ship were captured and the pirate crew put in irons, the "forced" men could claim their freedom as having been unwilling participants in all of the crimes perpetrated by the ship.

As for those who refused to serve and were not worth being "forced," they were sometimes made to walk the plank, though it was considered a favor to be shot rather than to endure the cruelty of the long walk into the abyss. Walking the plank, in which the victim was blindfolded and forced to walk on a board thrust out from the ship's side, was the source of amusement and sport. Pirates would place wagers on whether or not the victim would make it to the end of the plank or would lose his footing and fall off before reaching the end. In either case, of course, he fell into the water and drowned, or was eaten by sharks.

This practice, of walking the plank, originated in the days of the Roman Empire. The Mediterranean was then filled with pirates and when they captured a ship it was their habit to ask if there were any citizens of Rome on board. When the proud citizens came forward, thinking this distinction would afford them special treatment, the pirates would fall to their knees begging their pardon for any inconvenience they may have caused these noble Roman citizens. Then they would lead the prisoners to the side of the vessel and a waiting ladder. Still acting with the utmost courtesy, the pirates would again apologize for the mistake, and pointing to the ladder, explain that they were free to leave the ship. The catch was that there was no boat at the other end of the ladder. Horrified Romans realized their fate, as the pirates burst into screams of uncontrollable laughter and tossed them overboard to the death that had been intended for them all along. This hatred for authority, of which Rome was the ultimate representative of the time, has been characteristic of pirates down through the centuries.

SUPPLIES AND PROVISIONS

Provisioning the ship was as important an enterprise for pirate ships as it was for legal vessels. Food was usually easy to buy or steal from other ships and in various ports. Some ports were known to be pirate-friendly. But ammunition and armaments were not as easy to come by. It was, of course, illegal to furnish arms to pirates, but, as with everything where there is a potential profit, there are people willing to do business, no matter who the customer is or what they intend to do with the product.

There is an often repeated story about one navy captain who was sent out in pursuit of pirates on the coast of Madagascar. The captain informed his men that their ship had sprung a leak and needed immediate attention. In order to repair the bottom of the ship, it was necessary to off load the entire store of weaponry — powder, shot, and guns. The munitions were piled up on the beach. Afterwards all hands returned to the ship, careened farther down the beach. Oddly enough, there was no leak to be found. After some discussion, the ship was righted and a party of men sent to collect the munitions. To their surprise every single item had vanished. In their place were several small barrels, which the captain instructed them not to open but to deliver directly to his cabin. Obedience overcome by curiosity, the sailors opened the coffers and were amazed to find them filled with gold coins.

Oftentimes, merchant ships filled with brandy, rum, powder, pistols, and cannon ball would leave port with a legitimate customer for their wares and along the way put into some deserted island. There a pirate ship would take the entire cargo in exchange for silks, sugar, ivory, and odds and ends. In this manner the merchants had considerably shorter voyages and could quickly turn around to reload with more supplies. The only requirement was that the merchant captain not ask any questions about where the odd assortment of goods used to pay for the ammunition had come from.

On board a pirate ship it was usually feast or famine. One of the favorite dishes, was called salmagundi. The name is believed to come from the medieval French word *salemine*, meaning highly seasoned or salted. Its exact ingredients depended upon the cook and what food was available to him. Included might be any or all of the following: turtle meat, fish, pork, chicken, corned beef, ham, duck, and pigeon. The meats would be roasted, chopped into pieces and marinated in spiced wine, then mixed with cabbage, anchovies, pickled herring, mangoes, hard-boiled eggs, palm hearts, onions, olives, grapes, and any other pickled vegetables that were available. The entire concoction would then be highly seasoned with garlic, salt, pepper, and mustard seed and soaked with oil and vinegar — and naturally served with lots of beer and rum! So fond were the pirates of this meal that some vessels carried live turtles in the hold to be slaughtered and eaten while out on a long cruise.

When a pirate crew ate salmagundi things were going well. But normally the food eaten by pirates was atrocious. The water was fetid, the meat and fish rotten and the biscuits maggot infested. Many men could only eat in the dark so that they did not have to see what they were eating. Pirate crews were no strangers to starvation and thirst. Because of the unpredictable nature of sea travel, crews were often placed on critically small rations. This might explain the ferocity with which many pirate attacks were carried out. Men were likely to exhibit more bravery and fight harder when they were fighting not just for gold but to stave off starvation.

OPPOSITE — Frontispiece of the first Dutch edition of Captain Charles Johnson's *A General History of Pirates* (1726). Johnson's admirable history has served generations of writers. Some scholars question its reliablility, while others feel that in the main it is a fairly accurate account of the period and its fascinating cast of characters.Captain Johnson himself has been the subject of some dispute. In 1972 Manuel Schonhorn brought out a new edition of Johnson's *History*. In his introduction he claimed to have proved that Daniel Defoe was the actual author of the history, writing under a pseudonym. Defoe was clearly interested in pirates; he published a novel, *The King of Pirates* based on the life of Henry Every. Schonhorn believed that internal evidence further bolstered his argument. Recent scholarship has begun to challenge some of his assumptions, but the question remains an open one. This book draws freely from Johnson's work.

A Gallery of Pirates

HISTORIE DER ZEE-ROOVERS.

S.ʳ HEN: MORGAN

Portrait of Henry Morgan from Esquemelin's *Buccaneers of America*

Sir Henry Morgan

Sir Henry Morgan, often referred to as the greatest of all the "brethren of the coast," was a Welshman born at Llanrhymmy in Monmouthshire in the year 1635. The son of a well-to-do farmer, Robert Morgan, he took to seafaring at an early age. Morgan's only recorded words on this period of his life were, "I left school too young and have been more used to the pike than the book." As a young man Morgan went to Barbados, and afterwards settled in Jamaica. It is likely that he was part of the original expeditionary force sent by Cromwell to wrest the island from Spanish control. In any event it remained his home for the rest of his life.

The most thorough and colorful contemporary account of piracy, *The Buccaneers of America*, deals at great length with Morgan's exploits. Written originally in Dutch by the adventurer, Henri Esquemelin, who sailed with Morgan as a surgeon, the book was an immediate success. Translated into English it went through numerous editions. The portrait of Morgan that emerges from the book is that of a man of terrific energy and one possessed of great powers of persuasion. Esquemelin's depiction of Morgan's cruelty was probably exaggerated, though there is no doubt that he could be absolutely unscrupulous when it suited his ends. Morgan

OVERLEAF — Morgan's escape from the Maracaibo. At the bottom right the Spanish flagship *Magdalen* is being rammed by Morgan's fireship. From Esquemelin's *Buccaneers of America*.

actually sued William Crooke, the English publisher of the book, for libel. He made it clear, however, that he was more offended by the author's claiming that he had been kidnapped in Wales and sold, as a boy, into slavery, and sent to Barbados, than by any allegations of barbarism. As a result of this trial Crooke paid £200 damages to Morgan and published a long and groveling apology. Later editions of the book tone down the general character of the pirate.

Clearly Morgan saw himself as a patriot, out to defend the English Crown against the depredations of its most deadly enemy, Spain. He sailed as a privateer. But his behavior was at times indistinguishable from that of the most mercenary pirate. For example, when returning from his successful assault on the city of Panama in 1671, he left most of his faithful followers behind in Chagres, without ships or food, while he slipped off in the night with most of the booty to Jamaica.

Morgan served his apprenticeship with Sir Christopher Mings, an intrepid seaman who had commanded a ship during the invasion of Jamaica. Mings ravaged the Spanish Main and in an incredible stroke of good fortune stumbled upon a store of Spanish silver containing 1.5 million pieces of eight, an astronomical sum. The first document that mentions Morgan by name refers to Captain Henry Morgan as commander of one of ten ships sailing under letters of marque in Mings's admiralty.

Returning to Jamaica Morgan entered into partnership with the buccaneers Jackman and Morris, successfully plundered the coast of present day Central America, and returned once more a wealthy and highly regarded man. While he was away his uncle, Edward Morgan, had been named lieutenant governor of Jamaica, a post Henry Morgan later held. In the spring of 1665 Edward Morgan assumed command of an attack on the Dutch island of St. Eustatius. The exertion proved too much for him; he died of "surfeit" while pursuing the enemy. His nephew asked for the hand of his late uncle's daughter, Mary Elizabeth, and was married early in the following year.

Morgan now found himself in a uniquely favorable position. Married to one of the belles of island society and on friendly terms with the government, he was at the same time well-known and respected by the buccaneers who frequented the West Indies in search of booty.

In 1668, when he was 33 years old, Morgan was commissioned by the Jamaican government to gather together a force of privateers. Spain and England were again at war, and Morgan was made admiral of the fleet. His first sortie was an attack on the Cuban city of Puerto Principe. Unfortunately, the Spanish got wind of his plans and managed to hide most of their treasure. The attack netted him the negligible sum of 50,000 pieces of eight.

His next move proved more rewarding. He sailed for Portobello, a collection point for Spanish treasure on the Caribbean coast of Panama. With a combination of guile and courage he and his men took the city and spent 31 days in unrestrained looting. Warned by the local Indians, who hated the Spaniards, he was able to set an ambush for an expeditionary force that was sent overland to retake the town. He returned to Jamaica with spoils valued at more than £100,000 and was met with general rejoicing.

Although Morgan was becoming rich, his buccaneer companions were not faring nearly so well. At their urging he put to sea again with a motley fleet of twelve vessels. His flagship was a handsome frigate called the *Oxford*. One evening when Morgan was hosting a banquet for all the captains of his fleet, a sudden explosion gutted the ship. Practically the entire crew was killed. By a stroke of good luck Morgan and a few of his dinner guests survived.

Apparently unruffled by his close escape from death, Morgan seized a fine ship, the *Cour Volant*, from a French pirate, made her his own flagship, and christened her the *Satisfaction*. He then set off to raid the port of Maracaibo on the Gulf of Venezuela. Unknown to him, the Spanish had recently fortified the area. Once again his ability to rethink his strategy according to conditions on the ground served him well. He attacked by land and took the fort, and over the course of the next two months succeeded in divesting the inhabitants of almost £50,000 worth of silver and jewels. But now the Spanish fleet was out to get him. Three warships lay at the mouth of the only passage out of the gulf. Decisively outgunned, Morgan sent a ship right at the Spanish flagship, the *Magdalen*. The admiral confident in his superiority let it approach and prepared to board it, when all at once it exploded. The flames spread quickly to the *Magdalen*, and Morgan made his way into the channel and from there to a triumphant return to Jamaica.

Now Morgan began preparations for what was to be the greatest coup of his career — the sacking of Panama. Morgan's first action in the raid was to land a party that took the Castle of San Lorenzo at the mouth of the Chagres River. Morgan left a strong garrison there to cover his retreat and on January 9, 1671 pushed on up the river with 1,400 men in a fleet of canoes. The journey across the isthmus, through the tropical jungle, was very hard on the men, particularly as they, expecting to find provisions to supply their needs along the way, had carried no food with them. They practically starved until the sixth day, when they stumbled across a barn full of maize that the fleeing Spanish had neglected to destroy. On the evening of the ninth day a scout reported he had seen the steeple of a church in Panama. Morgan, with that touch of genius that so often brought him success, attacked the city from a direction the Spanish had not thought possible, so their guns were all placed where they were useless. They were compelled to do just what the buccaneer leader wanted them to do — namely, to come out of their fortifications and fight him in the open. The battle raged fiercely for two hours between the brave Spanish defenders and the equally brave but nearly exhausted buccaneers.

When at last the Spanish turned and ran, the buccaneers were too tired to immediately follow up their success. But after a brief rest they advanced, and at the end of three hours of street fighting the city was theirs. The first thing Morgan now did was to assemble all his men and strictly forbid them to drink any wine, telling them that he had secret information that the wine had been poisoned by the Spanish before they left the city. This was, of course, a scheme of Morgan's to stop his men from becoming drunk, when they would be at the mercy of the enemy should they return to attempt to retake the city.

Morgan now set about plundering the city, a large part of which was burnt to the ground, though whether this was done on his orders or by the fleeing Spanish governor has never been established. After three weeks the buccaneers started back on their journey to San Lorenzo, with a troop of 200 pack mules laden with gold, silver, and goods of all sorts, together with a large number of prisoners. The rearguard of the march was under the command of a relative of the admiral, Colonel Bledry Morgan.

On their arrival at Chagres the spoils were divided, amidst a great deal of fighting, and in March 1671, Morgan sailed off to Port Royal, Jamaica, with a few friends and the greater part of the plunder, leaving his followers behind without ships or provisions, and with only £10 per person as their share of the spoils.

On May 31, 1671, the Jamaican legislature passed a vote of thanks to Morgan for his successful expedition, and this in spite of the fact that in July of the preceding year a treaty had been concluded at Madrid between Spain and England for "restraining depredations and establishing peace" in the New World. The political winds were changing and with them Morgan's fortunes. His friend, the governor, was removed from power, and in order to appease the Spanish court, Morgan was placed under arrest.

In April 1672 Morgan was carried to England as a prisoner on board the frigate *Welcome*. But because of his enormous popularity he was never incarcerated or convicted.

In fact, he passed much of his time in London consulting with high government officials, and in 1674 he was knighted and returned to Jamaica, this time as lieutenant governor.

Morgan was a man of action and a "normal" life ashore proved tiresome to him. We learn from a 1674 report sent home by the governor, Lord Vaughan, that Morgan "frequented the taverns of Port Royal, drinking and gambling in unseemly fashion." But nevertheless the Jamaica assembly voted the lieutenant governor a sum of £600 as a special salary, hardly a sign of disfavor. In 1676 Vaughan brought definite charges against Morgan and another member of the government, Robert Byndloss, of giving aid to certain Jamaican pirates. Morgan made a spirited defense and, no doubt owing largely to his popularity, got off, and in 1678 was granted a commission as captain of a company of 100 men.

The Towne of Puerto del Principe taken & sackt

Morgan's attack on Puerto Principe from Esquemelin's *Buccaneers of America.*

49

The Sacking of Panama, a colorful depiction by Howard Pyle.

The governor who succeeded Vaughan was Lord Carlisle. Carlisle seems to have had a soft spot for Morgan, in spite of his jovial "goings on" with his old buccaneer friends in the taverns of Port Royal. Carlisle speaks in his letters of Morgan's "generous Manner," and hints that despite whatever allowances are settled on him "he will be a beggar."

In 1681 Sir Thomas Lynch was appointed governor, and trouble at once began between him and his deputy. Among the charges the former brought against Morgan was one of having been overheard to say, "God damn the Assembly!" for which he was suspended from that body.

In April 1688 the king, at the urgent request of the Duke of Albemarle, ordered Morgan to be reinstated to the Assembly, but Morgan did not live long to enjoy his restored honors — he died on August 25, 1688.

An extract from the journal of Captain Lawrence Wright, commander of H.M.S. *Assistance*, dated August 1688, describes the burial ceremonies for Morgan held at Port Royal that show how important and popular a man he was. It states:

Saturday 25. This day at about noon Sir Henry Morgan died, & the 26th was brought over from Passage-fort to the King's house at Port Royall, from thence to the Church, & after a sermon was carried to the Pallisades & there buried. All the forts fired an equal number of guns, wee fired two & twenty & after wee & the Drake had fired, all the merchantmen had fired.

Morgan's will, which was filed in the Record Office at Spanish Town, apparently made provisions for his wife and near relatives. He was given a hero's burial.

Bartholomew Roberts

If the success of a pirate is measured by the damage he inflicted and the amount of booty he amassed, there can be no question that Captain Bartholomew Roberts deserves to be placed at the very head of his profession. He is said to have taken more than 400 vessels. The only man who can be said to have rivaled him was Henry Morgan. But Morgan, although in some ways an unmitigated blackguard, was motivated by patriotic sentiments. Roberts was a thorough man of business; he felt no such compunctions.

Roberts, like many other of his fellow freebooters, was born in Wales, not far from Haverfordwest. He was described as a tall, dark-complexioned man and was a most atypical pirate. First of all, he drank only tea — thus being the only total abstainer known to the fraternity. Also, he was a strict disciplinarian. Aboard his ship all lights had to be extinguished by 8:00 p.m.; any of the crew who wished to continue drinking after that hour had to do so on the open deck regardless of the weather. He allowed no women on his ships; in fact, one of his articles stated that any man who brought a woman aboard disguised as a man was to be executed. Also, he allowed no games of cards or dice to be played for money since he was strongly opposed to gambling.

OPPOSITE — Contemporary engraving of Roberts elaborately costumed with dreaded pirate flag in the background (Library of Congress).

53

Bartholomew Roberts at Whydah. The three-masted vessel in the foreground was his flagship at the time, the *Royal Fortune* (Peabody Essex Museum, Salem, Mass.).

He was a strict observer of the Sabbath and allowed even the ships' musicians, who, according to custom, were literally at the beck and call of the crew, to have a day of rest on Sunday.

Roberts used to place a guard on any women prisoners aboard his ship. It is perhaps not surprising that there was always fierce competition among the crew members for this duty. All quarrels had to be settled on shore, pirate fashion, the duelists standing back to back armed with pistol and cutlass. Roberts tolerated no fighting among the crew while on board his ship.

Roberts must have cut a striking figure and looked every bit the pirate when dressed for action. He used to wear a rich damask waistcoat and breeches, a red feather in his cap, a gold chain around his neck with a huge diamond cross hanging from it, a sword in his hand, and two pairs of pistols hanging at the end of a silk sling flung over his shoulders.

In November 1719 at a young age, Roberts set sail from London aboard the *Princess*, a merchant vessel. This was attacked and taken by the Welsh pirate Howell Davis, who commanded a vessel named the *Rover*. Though at first Roberts seemed reluctant to embark on this new career, he soon changed his mind. After only six weeks of service, Captain Davis was killed in an action against a Portuguese warship, and the crew elected Roberts as their new captain.

Roberts's speech to his fellow pirates was short but to the point. He said "that since he had dipped his hands in muddy water, and must be a pirate, it was better being a commander than a common man." Though this was not the most tactful way of expressing his gratitude, it was undoubtedly understood by his audience.

Roberts began his career as captain in dramatic fashion. To avenge the death of his former captain he seized and razed the fort at Anamaboe on the coast of Guinea, bombarded the town, and burned two Portuguese ships before sailing away the same night.

Sailing to Brazil he found a fleet of forty-two Portuguese ships laden with goods and precious cargo ready to set sail for Lisbon. Roberts, with incredible temerity, sailed right in among the Portuguese ships and, iden-tifying the most heavily laden of them, attacked and boarded her, even though his was a much smaller ship. He took the plunder and sailed away from the Portuguese fleet practically before they realized what had hap-pened. Among the treasures liberated was a cross of diamonds designed for the king of Portugal. It was this prized ornament that he would wear into battle.

This type of daring action, typical of Roberts, combined with his cool head and his insistence on discipline, accounts for his extraordinary suc-cess. His first important prize was rich indeed. In addition to the ship itself, Roberts took £30,000 worth of gold coins and other rich cargo. However, Roberts was betrayed and both the *Rover* and his prize were stolen by Walter Kennedy, the lieutenant he left in charge while he was off in a captured sloop.

Roberts renamed this ten-gun sloop the *Fortune*. With the *Fortune* Roberts seized an eighteen-gun galley and then traded her for a twenty-eight-gun French ship, renaming each in turn the *Royal Fortune*. Many seaman on the captured ships enlisted voluntarily and the pirates recruit-ed others by force. Roberts preferred English sailors and reports state that he tortured and killed French captives.

In the summer of 1720, due to an error in navigation Roberts and his crew wound up far from their destination of Brava — one of the Cape Verde Islands. Although sailors of the day could take latitudinal mea-surements with a fair degree of accuracy, it was not until later in the cen-

Sir Chalconer Ogle, commander of H.M.S. *Swallow,* the ship that captured the *Royal Fortune.* From a contemporary print. Artist unknown.

tury that a method was discovered for establishing a ship's longitude. Navigators often had little idea of how far east or west they were. Roberts' fleet changed its course for the port of Surinam, but that was more than 2,000 miles away, and they only had one casket of water for the whole crew of 124 men.

Water was rationed down to one mouthful per person per day. In order to mitigate their thirst, some men ate only a crust of bread a day. Some drank salt water, but that only increased their thirst and in the end drove them mad. The ones who did not eat were almost too weak to work. Somehow, they survived, and eventually the *Royal Fortune* dropped anchor off the Maroni River, on the coast of Surinam, in Dutch Guyana. Here they got much needed water and were able to rest and prepare to take to the open sea again.

Roberts was just about to capture a ship off St. Kitts when he learned of an expedition that had been sent out against him by the governor of Martinique. The idea that anyone would dare thwart his purposes enraged him. He ordered a new black flag to be made adorned with a portrait of himself standing with each foot planted on a skull, one of which was labeled "A.B.H.," the other "A.M.H.," signifying respectively, "A Barbadian's Head" and "A Martinican's Head."

Next they traveled to Bonnet's Key, in the Bay of Hispaniola, where they careened their ship and spent the rest of their time drinking. There was so much rum that any man who remained sober was frowned upon, and, with the exception of Roberts himself, was looked upon with suspicion. Harry Glasby learned this the hard way. He had been forced to join Roberts' company but because he had a good knowledge of navigation had been made one of the mates of the *Royal Fortune*. One day when the whole crew was asleep or dazed with rum, Glasby, who hated being a pirate, and two companions ran away into the woods, where they hoped to hide until the pirates put to sea.

However, they were soon missed — their very sobriety had aroused misgivings among the crew — and a hunt was instituted. The three men were soon found and returned to the ship where they were placed in irons while a court assembled to try them. Glasby was acquitted but his two companions were executed that very afternoon.

After this episode Roberts returned to the coast of Africa where he took many French ships, including two warships sent from France to protect their commercial shipping against just such men as Roberts.

While doing business along the Gold Coast a great atrocity was perpetrated by the men of Roberts' crew, although Roberts was not really to blame. Roberts had captured eleven ships at one time at Whydah, while their captains were all on shore doing business. When he offered to ransom them back, the French and English agreed to his terms. A Portuguese captain refused. The Portuguese ship *Porcupine* had already been partially loaded with slaves. Roberts ordered his men to board the vessel, free

The *Swallow* catches the *Royal Fortune* by surprise. From Johnson's
A General History of Pirates (Rare Books Division, The New York Public
Library, Astor, Lenox, and Tilden Foundations).

the slaves and then set the ship on fire to teach the Portuguese a lesson. In
their haste for destruction his men did not follow his orders and set fire to
the ship immediately upon boarding her. The slaves, who lay in the hold
chained two by two had no choice but to perish in the flames or jump into
the sea, where the sharks made as certain an end of them as the flames did
of those who remained on board. In all eighty slaves died.

While this was going on, two English men-of-war, the *Swallow* and
the *Weymouth* were cruising up and down the long strip of the mainland
that was their patrol, looking for pirates. The ships they encountered told
of the atrocities committed at every port from Sierra Leone to Old
Calabar.

On February 5, 1722, Roberts sighted the *Swallow* and took her, from
a distance, to be a merchant ship. He sent the *Ranger*, one of his consorts,
in pursuit. When they came within range of her guns, the pirates hoisted
the black flag. None of them had any clue that the prize was actually a

British man-of-war. Some thought she was a Portuguese trader loaded with sugar, while others swore she was a slaver. All doubts were dispelled as they came nearer. The *Swallow* suddenly let fly a broadside. Caught unawares, the pirates first of all struck their colors to signify surrender, but then sheared off and started to fight again. Soon the pirates realized that they were overmatched and their resistance wilted. Again they struck their colors and this time allowed a party from the *Swallow* to board them. When the *Ranger* was taken by the English her crew consisted of 77 Englishmen, 16 Frenchmen and 20 Africans. While the English were clambering aboard the pirates wrapped their black flag around several cannon ball and hoisted it overboard so that it could not be used as evidence against them. The prisoners were all securely placed in irons and stowed in the hold while the *Swallow* went in pursuit of the *Royal Fortune* and Captain Roberts.

When the *Swallow* was spotted by the lookout on the *Royal Fortune*, Roberts came on deck. He was every inch the gallant pirate. Running close to the *Swallow* he hoisted his black flag, received the man-of-war's broadside and returned it.

A sudden change of wind allowed the *Swallow* to move dangerously close to the *Royal Fortune*. She fired a second broadside and with a thunderous roar grape-shot and cannon-balls whizzed across the pirate deck. A piece of metal struck Roberts in the throat and he fell to the deck without a word. He died instantly. As the battle raged on two of his crew ran to him and grabbing him by the arms heaved their captain overboard, as he had told them to do if ever he died in battle. He preferred being fed to the sharks than being hung in chains, as was sometimes done with the bodies of notorious pirates.

With the death of Roberts the pirates lost all enthusiasm for the fight and they were defeated by the English. Nearly all were found guilty and hanged outside Cape Coast Castle, where they swung in the hot sun of the Gold Coast for many days.

FRANCIS LOLONOIS.

Portrait of François l'Olonnais from Esquemelin's *Buccaneers of America*

Captain Nau

Jean David Nau, also known as François l'Olonnais, was one of the most ruthless and barbaric pirates ever to sail under the Jolly Roger.

Born in France, he was sent, while still a child, as an indentured servant to the French island of Martinique in the West Indies. After completing his term of servitude l'Olonnais moved onto the island of Hispaniola (shared at the present day by Haiti and the Dominican Republic) and joined the buccaneers there. These free spirits subsisted on the dried flesh of the wild cattle they hunted.

L'Olonnais signed on as a sailor and acted with such ability and courage that the governor of Tortuga Island, Monsieur de la Place, gave him the command of a vessel and sent him out to seek his fortune.

At first the young buccaneer was very successful, and he captured many Spanish ships. But his unusually ferocious treatment of prisoners earned him a reputation for cruelty that has never been surpassed. At the height of these early successes his ship was wrecked by a storm off the Yucatan. Most of his crew managed to get ashore, where they were immediately attacked by a group of Spaniards. L'Olonnais was the only one to survive. The cunning captain escaped by smearing blood and sand all over his face and body and hiding himself among his fallen comrades on the beach. Disguised as a Spaniard, he entered the city of Campeche, which was alit with bonfires in celebration of the news that their dreaded enemy had finally been killed.

Meeting with some French slaves, l'Olonnais contrived a plan to escape by canoe. Under the cover of nightfall the small band crept out of the fortified town eventually returning to Tortuga, a pirate stronghold of the time. Here the entrepreneurial young captain stole a small vessel and started out once again "on the account," plundering a small village in Cuba called de Los Cagos. When the governor of Havana received word

The Cruelty of Lolonois
LOLONOIS

of the notorious and apparently resurrected pirate's arrival, he sent a well-armed ship to take him with orders to hang all the crew with the exception of l'Olonnais, who was to be brought back to Havana alive and in chains. But l'Olonnais outmaneuvered his pursuers. He boarded the Spanish vessel and with his able gang of cutthroats murdered the entire crew with the exception of one poor soul who was sent back to the governor bearing word that in the future l'Olonnais would kill any Spaniard with whom he came in contact.

Joining with the famous freebooter Michel de Basco, l'Olonnais soon organized a more ambitious expedition, consisting of a fleet of eight vessels and 400 men. Sailing to the Gulf of Venezuela in 1667, they destroyed the fort that guarded its entrance. Next they sailed to the port of Maracaibo where they found that all the inhabitants had fled in terror. The pirates tracked down many of the refugees who were hiding in the nearby woods. There l'Olonnais killed large numbers of them in an attempt to force them to disclose the hiding places of their treasures. Their next move was to march upon the town of Gibraltar, which was gallantly defended by the Spanish, who, after suffering the loss of 500 killed, eventually surrendered. For weeks the inhabitants of this town lived a waking nightmare. Rape, murder, and pillage were daily occurrences. Finally, to the great relief of the miserable inhabitants, l'Olonnais sailed away with cargo holds of booty to Corso Island, a rendezvous of the French buccaneers. Here they divided the profits of their enterprise, which amounted to the vast sum of 260,000 pieces of eight, as well as large stocks of silverplate, silk and jewels. A share was also allotted to the next of kin of those who had died, and extra shares were given to those who had lost either an eye or a limb, in accordance with the company's articles.

By now the name l'Olonnais had become infamous up and down the coast of the Spanish Main. Never satisfied, l'Olonnais began planning an even more daring expedition. Drawn by rumors of great wealth he set out for the coast of Nicaragua. Here he continued his reign of terror, committing the most atrocious acts of violence on the Spanish inhabitants. One story graphically illustrates how the term bloodthirsty became indissolubly linked with the word pirate. During an attack on the town San Pedros, the pirates were ambushed and many of them killed. The tide of the battle eventually turned and the Spaniards were forced to take flight. Most of the captured Spaniards were killed but a few were kept alive to be questioned by l'Olonnais in order to find an alternate and undefended route to the town. Frustrated with the prisoners' silence, l'Olonnais drew his cutlass and with it cut open the chest of one of the Spaniards. He then

OPPOSITE — The cruelty of L'Olonnais from Esquemelin's *Buccaneers of America*.

63

pulled out his still beating heart and began to gnaw and bite at it like a ravenous wolf, saying to the other prisoners, "I will serve you all alike if you show me not another way."

Shortly after this, perhaps fearing reprisals or maybe just finally questioning the sanity of their captain, many of his crew broke away and sailed off on their own; not so much a mutiny as a wholesale defection. L'Olonnais sailed for the coast of Honduras and ran his vessel on a sand bank and lost her. Stranded on the Las Pertas Islands, he needed six months to build and outfit another vessel. L'Olonnais had plans to sail for Cartagena but never realized them. He was caught by the native Indians, and as described by the writer Esquemelin, "Here suddenly his ill-fortune assailed him, which of a long time had been reserved for him as a punishment due to the multitude of horrible crimes, which in his horrible and licentious life he had committed. For God Almighty, the time of His divine justice now already come, had appointed the Indians of Darien to be the instruments and the executioners thereof."

These "instruments of God," having captured l'Olonnais, tore him in pieces alive, throwing his body limb by limb into the fire and his ashes into the air so that "no trace nor memory might remain of such an infamous inhuman creature." It has been said that had l'Olonnais lived in the present day he would certainly have been confined to an asylum for the mentally ill.

Captain Thomas Tew

Thomas Tew was a famous pirate, whose headquarters was at Madagascar. He was mentioned by name as a specially "wicked and ill-disposed person" in King William III's 1695 Royal Warrant to Captain Kidd, which commissioned him to hunt for pirates.

Tew sailed in consort with Captain Dew from Barbados in 1692 with a commission from the governor to join with the Royal African Company in an attack on the French factory at Goori, in Gambia. But instead of going to West Africa, Tew and his crew turned pirates and sailed to the Red Sea. There he encountered a richly provisioned Indian ship and promptly attacked. Prevailing in the battle, he took her as a prize. The booty was so rich that each man of Tew's crew received £3,000 as his share. Laden with this new-found wealth, they sailed to Madagascar.

Tew was soon held in high esteem by the pirates who resided in that favorite stronghold. There are some questions as to the subsequent course of Tew's career. What follows is based on the account in Captain Johnson's, *A General History of Pirates*. According to Johnson it was at this time that Tew met the legendary pirate French pirate Misson, in his garden city of Libertalia. (Contemporary scholars have questioned the existence of both Misson and Libertalia.) Johnson portrays Misson as a thoroughly idealistic pirate whose ship was run upon republican principles. His career is said to have culminated with the founding of Libertalia, a pirate utopia. A quarrel arose between Misson's French followers and Tew's English pirates. A duel was arranged between the two leaders, but by the tact and intervention of another pirate — a defrocked Italian priest — all was settled amicably. Tew was appointed Admiral and the diplomatic ex-priest suitably chosen as Secretary of State to the little republic. Tew had such a reputation for kindness that ships seldom resisted him; upon learning who their assailant was they gave themselves up freely.

Around this time some of Tew's men sailed off to start a colony on their own. The Admiral followed trying to persuade them to return to the

fold at Libertalia. The men refused, and while Tew was arguing with them, his ship was lost in a sudden and fierce storm. Tew was soon rescued by the ship *Bijoux* with Misson on board, who, with a few men had narrowly escaped being massacred by the natives.

Tew must have realized that the eastern waters were becoming less hospitable to pirates. Furnished with an equal share of gold and diamonds from Misson's last venture, he made his way to back to America and settled down in Rhode Island. Tew was now a wealthy man. With an honesty rarely encountered in those who pursued his trade, he kept a promise to his friends in Bermuda, who had originally set him up with a ship, and sent them fourteen times the original cost of the sloop as their share of the profits.

In the end Tew found the call of the sea and the lure of the grand account irresistible. He consented to take command of a pirate ship en route to the Red Sea. Soon after his arrival, Tew attacked a large ship belonging to the Great Mogul and during the battle was mortally wounded. His biographer tells us " a shot carried away the rim of Tew's belly, who held his bowels with his hands for some space. When he dropped, it struck such terror to his men that they suffered themselves to be taken without further resistance." Thus fell fighting a fine sailor, a brave man, and a successful pirate, and one who cheated the gallows awaiting him at Execution Dock.

OPPOSITE — Thomas Tew taking his ease with New York's Governor Fletcher. Howard Pyle.

Henry Every, arch-pirate. From Johnson's *A General History of Pirates*.

Henry Every

Known as "Long Ben" to his associates, Every was in his time called "the Arch Pirate." He earned this moniker by seizing two treasure ships belonging to the Great Mogul of India, which greatly excited the public's interest and imagination back in England. This turned out to be one of the richest hauls in the history of piracy and had serious repercussions on legitimate trading done by European companies.

Every's admirers invented improbable stories about his early life. He is first mentioned in the early 1690s as an unlicensed slave dealer and pirate sailing from the Bahamas and enjoying the protection of the governor. In June 1694, Every was second in command of a 46-gun private warship, licensed by the Spanish government to harass, attack, and capture French smugglers based on Martinique. One evening when the captain was dead drunk, the crew turned pirate and took the ship. Renaming her the *Fancy,* they elected Every to be their captain.

Heading south along the African coast, the pirates plundered three British vessels in the Comoros Islands, northwest of Madagascar. There Every seized a French pirate ship loaded with Moorish treasure, and most of the French pirates signed Every's articles, joining his crew.

Before leaving the Comoros port of Johanna, Every composed a letter addressed to all English commanders, which eventually reached London and was printed in the newspapers. It read:

I was riding her in the Fancy, man-of-war, formerly the Charles of the Spanish expedition . . . being then and now a ship of 46 guns, 150 men, and bound to seek our fortunes. I have never yet wronged any English or Dutch, nor ever intend whilst I am commander. . . . If you or any whom you may inform are desirous to know what we are at a distance, then make your ancient [ensign] up in a ball or bundle and hoist him at the mizen peak, the mizen being furled. I shall answer with the same, and never molest you, but my men are hungry, stout, and resolute, and should they exceed my desire I cannot help myself . . .

As yet an Englishman's friend

— Henry Every

This letter seemed incredibly brazen to some, while others deemed it the righteous act of a loyal Englishman. It is indisputable, however, that it established Every's reputation. People were fond of speculating on where he would strike next, and whether or not he would ever be captured.

Reaching the Red Sea in June 1695, Every found the waters crowded with pirates. Present in the area were ships commanded by William Want, Joseph Farrell, William May, Thomas Wake, and Thomas Tew. Every organized them into a navy of sorts and placed himself in command as a pirate admiral. The newly assembled and organized fleet lay in wait for the treasure ships belonging to the Mogul of India that returned every year at this time filled with gold and silver after trading the silks and other luxury goods native to India.

Finally the pirates spotted their prey. As it turned out, most of the Indian ships were able to escape under the cover of nightfall, but the rising sun proved to be Every's best ally. As it rose it exposed the last two vessels trying to sneak past. The smaller of the two, the *Fateh Mohammed*, put up little struggle and was easily captured. However, the *Gang-i-sawai (Gunsway)* was obviously well armed and prepared to offer a determined resistance. The *Gunsway* turned out to be the largest ship in the entire Indian fleet, and carried 450 soldiers. Every pursued her until close enough to engage her. During a fierce battle, which lasted two hours, both sides suffered heavy casualties.

In those days it was considered normal for whites to brutalize people of color, since they were considered heathens anyway. However, history records that Every and his crew acted with particular barbarity in their treatment of the Indian prisoners and especially of some Turkish girls who were being transported to India. Many of the girls later died from the injuries resulting from their being brutally raped. Men and women alike were tortured to make them confess to the whereabouts of hidden treasures on the ship. Some of the women leapt overboard to their deaths, and others killed themselves with daggers rather than submit to the pirates.

Contemporary engraving of Every being waited on as befit a pirate of his estate (Library of Congress).

Henry Every negotiating with a London merchant over the price of some treasure. Howard Pyle.

The *Gunsway* turned out to contain treasure beyond Every's wildest dreams. From the ship were taken large quantities of gold, silver, and jewels, including a saddle set with rubies intended as a present for the Great Mogul. The Indian owners later estimated their losses at £600,000.

When Every divided the loot among his crew and the crews of the other ships in his little fleet, each man received more than £1,000 plus a quantity of jewels. The pirates had now made their fortunes and the fleet disbanded. The ships scattered in every direction. Every wanted to return to New Providence, but many of his crew wanted to head for Brazil, and there was very nearly a mutiny. In the end Every got his way.

The pirates took a leisurely cruise across the Atlantic until finally they reached New Providence. Governor Trott, royal governor of the Bahamas, a corrupt a man as ever lived, personally welcomed Every and his crew. Of course he had good reason to rejoice at their recent success.

He was paid a total of £7,000 in money and goods in exchange for his protection.

Now that they were rich men, Every's crew had no taste for returning to sea. Their problem was that they could not return to England. Although they were enjoying Trott's protection on New Providence, they were liable to be arrested and hanged if they set foot in England or any other British colony. Some of the them slipped secretly into the North American colonies and took up quiet lives. Others, even though they knew that they were wanted criminals in England, decided to try to return to their homeland. There they hoped to live like gentlemen with their new fortunes. The trouble was that the pirates were not raised as gentlemen and could not help but attract attention to themselves. Because they were so unused to having and handling large sums of money they made themselves quite noticeable in England. They threw money around with abandon. In London and Bristol jewelers and goldsmiths reported strange sailors selling foreign coins and precious gems, and in this way Every's crew was rounded up one at a time. In all 24 of his men were arrested. Six were eventually hanged and most of the rest were deported to Virginia as convict laborers.

Every, however, proved to be not only the "Arch Pirate" but also a master criminal. He was never apprehended. After arriving in Ireland he dropped out of sight and was never heard from again. Many stories circulated reporting his many different whereabouts from Scotland to Wales to Ireland. Every sightings were as common then as Elvis sightings are today. Daniel Defoe's novel, *King of the Pirates,* written in the 1720s, was a thinly disguised fictional account of Every's career.

Every's exploits left him a rich and greatly envied man; but aside from that, they had some serious consequences. First, the East India Company suffered heavily from the wrath of the Mogul rulers of India. The company was forced to close down many of its trading posts in that country. Anti-English sentiments ran high due not just to the attack but because of the incredible cruelty with which the victims were treated. Second, Every did more than perhaps any other pirate to encourage men to dream about being, and no doubt in many cases actually become, pirates. Not only was Every wildly successful, he escaped punishment for his crimes. It was the fantasy of every lowly seaman. The thought of Every's vanishing to live the life of a squire must have inspired many men to piracy.

Nassau town — New Providence Island — Bahamas, 1718.
William Gilkerson (By kind permission of the artist).

Pirate Strongholds

In the early eighteenth century there was a saying that when pirates dreamed they had died and gone to heaven, they dreamed of the island of New Providence in the Bahamas.

This island, the present day Nassau, was infested with pirates and had everything to make it the ideal haven for those who sought to stay as far as possible from the law. The harbor was protected by a small island lying off the main one and provided two ways in and out, so that no single ship could trap a pirate ship inside the bay.

The climate was warm enough in winter for the simplest shelter rigged from a sail, and yet pleasant in summer due to the cooling trade winds. The hills behind the beach provided a sweeping view of the horizon, where lookouts could keep watch for potential victims wending their way among the islands of the Bahamas. The pirates erected a fort on the long low island forming the harbor. It commanded the only passage deep enough for any warship, creating an invulnerable anchorage.

Just one hundred yards in back of the white sand beach lay a tangled jungle where no pursuer could ever find his fleeing quarry. In short, it would be hard to imagine a more tactically secure pirate headquarters.

Even more important, since pirates were not by nature defensive creatures, the island was the perfect base to launch attacks. The Bahamas lay directly on the trade routes from the New World to the Old. The lumbering trader bound from Port Royal to England, the New England schooner heading home from Cuba with her cargo of rum, the amazingly rich Spanish plate fleet en route to Madrid from the silver mines of South America — all ran through or past the Bahamas. All ships who wished to trade in these waters knew that they were running the risk of encountering pirates.

From New Providence it was only a few hours sail to the great highways of the Caribbean; the Straits of Florida, Windward Passage, Providence Channels, and Mona Passage. Pirates could, and often did, slip in behind one of the thousands of low, sandy cays and pounce upon the passing merchantmen as they sailed up the coast of Florida. The strong currents of the Gulf Stream run through this area and few ships of that period could successfully put about and evade an attacking ship when the pirates were closing in for the kill. Ship after ship sailed into the ambush, providing a rich harvest for the bands of pirates.

To the untrained eye it was difficult to distinguish between temporary and permanent quarters on New Providence. The Nassau of today, a luxurious destination for jet-setters and holiday seekers from all over the world, was in the early eighteenth century a sprawling, brawling tent city that would have made the worst cow town of the American Wild West look tame by comparison. There were no buildings to speak of on the entire island. Most "structures" consisted of spars in the sand with ragged sails tossed over them. Tents were pitched wherever the "builder" pleased, resulting in a maze of tents connected by narrow, winding paths. A few scattered wells provided water, and toilet facilities were typically behind the nearest bush. The more fastidious inhabitants carried their trash and garbage down to the water's edge. The rest, the overwhelming majority, simply tossed everything out the tent door and let it rot in the broiling tropical sun. When the wind was strong, it was said that out on the ocean you could smell New Providence before you could see it.

Pirates have always been closely connected to tales of drunkenness and songs of rum. Nowhere were pirates more at home in their debauchery than on New Providence. It seems there was one tavern keeper for every dozen or so pirates. There was no red-light district as such because none was necessary; the whores, of all ages and colors, were everywhere. By day the town was chaos. Peddlers shouted their way in and out of the tents, selling fish, conch, bananas, coconuts, and papayas. Gangs of children followed the hawkers, dogging them and attempting to sample their wares free of charge. Women screeched at youngsters who toddled in the filth, while babies cried and dogs fought. Parrots shrieked obscenities painstakingly taught to them by amused owners. Drunks staggered from one tavern to another or stumbled to the waterfront to relieve themselves or to stretch out in the sand for a nap. At nightfall the action shifted to the taverns. Indulging their taste for rum, the pirates gambled and caroused with the practitioners of a trade older even than piracy. Night was the best time in New Providence. It shrouded the dumping grounds around the tents. Candles and lanterns glowed softly from the tavern windows, in the tents, and on the pirate ships riding at anchor in the harbor.

The relative peace and quiet of the night could be broken at any moment by the arrival of a pirate ship. For pirates who had been at

The Burning Ship. Charlie Vane escaped from New Providence by setting fire
to a ship and directing it at Woodes Rogers' fleet. Howard Pyle.

Drunken brawls were frequent occurences in the taverns of New Providence.
N. C. Wyeth.

sea, the joy of arriving at New Providence was overwhelming. Few, if any, could refrain from expressing their delight in as loud a manner as possible. The story is told of one pirate who preferred not to drink alone. He regularly bought a large quantity of wine upon his arrival on the island. Positioning himself at the center of town he would offer a drink to any passerby who struck his fancy. If the recipient demurred, the pirate shot him.

Other pirates who were "on the town" staged drinking marathons, stumbling from tavern to tavern. The last man on his feet was declared the winner. In similar marathons women sometimes took the place of wine. A pirate on shore leave in New Providence generally followed a pattern: the first night he spent drinking himself into oblivion. When he awoke, sometime late in the second day, he found a woman companion for the second night's drinking. By the third or fourth day he settled down to steady gambling and drinking which lasted as long as his share of the loot held out. Most pirates quit only when their funds were exhausted in one last drunken orgy. They were usually carried aboard for the next cruise.

New Providence was indeed a tropical paradise for the pirates. However, to the government at home in England, striving to keep order in the New World and to protect the all-important trade routes, this island was thought of as the cesspool of the Western Hemisphere. Only on the tiny island of Saint Mary's near Madagascar, off the eastern coast of Africa, was there a comparable pirate stronghold; and some of Madagascar's most formidable pirates received their basic training at New Providence.

In the history of the Bahamas, and New Providence in particular, no one had ever made such good use of the islands as the pirates. The English settlement on New Providence, after nearly a century of just hanging on, failed. The Spanish captured the island and shortly gave it up as worthless, leaving the British colonists free to move back in. Just after the turn of the eighteenth century a pirate named Captain Henry Jennings discovered the unique usefulness of the island. He and his crew simply took over. By word of mouth the special piratical advantages of the island spread through the transient freebooter communities of the other West Indian islands. Within a decade the pirate capital of New Providence was in full flower.

From their New Providence base pirate ships spread out not only all through the Caribbean but to Bermuda and up the North American coast as far as New England as well. The effect on merchant shipping was disastrous. Insurance rates rose to the point of diminishing returns. Local governors, unable to cope with either the pirates or the very unhappy merchants, convinced London to send greater naval aid to the area. But their task was not an easy one. Arriving, the British faced several problems. Many sailors, unused to the tropics, became ill. Others, disenchanted with their harsh lives in the Royal Navy, deserted and joined the pirates. As shipping was more and more affected, out-of-work sailors made their way to New Providence, swelling the number of inhabitants and providing a large camp of unemployed, eager men for the captains who were always looking for fresh recruits to become brethren of the coast.

The situation deteriorated to the point that a person traveling to or from the West Indies or even from one island to another was literally risking his life. The governors of the colonies were completely unable to deal with as large and fierce an enemy as the pirates of New Providence. In concert with the Admiralty they came to the conclusion that the island had to be cleaned out, and the waters of the Caribbean once again made safe for travel and commerce. Doing this, however, was more easily decided upon than accomplished.

In London the ministers of King George I decided on a two-pronged offensive. First, the king would issue a proclamation of amnesty, officially called The King's Act of Grace, granting pardon to all pirates who gave themselves up within a stipulated time. Though the amnesty was not entirely effective, it did attract a certain number of pirates. An added benefit was that among the pirates who did take advantage of the king's pardon, there were always some who were willing to supply information as to the whereabouts and strength of colleagues they particularly disliked.

But many pirates scoffed at the idea of giving up their entirely satisfactory way of life, and many who took the pardon would, after a rest period, go "on the account" again. Thus the second prong of the king's offensive was the eradication of those who continued recalcitrant. The Admiralty chose Woodes Rogers, the ideal man for this unenviable task. Rogers' orders called for him to clean up New Providence and the entire Bahamas. He was given a small force of troops and three warships. Rogers took his job very seriously and actually spent a whole year preparing before setting sail from England.

When the proclamation of amnesty was officially announced, the governor of Bermuda quickly dispatched a copy to New Providence. Captain Pearse, in command of H.M.S. *Phoenix*, delivered the news personally to the pirates of New Providence. His reception was less than cordial. He was told in no uncertain terms to up anchor and make haste or his ship would be burned under him. The frustrated and angered captain wrote to his superiors that the pirates "showed no small hatred to government."

When Woodes Rogers arrived in June 1718 with his little fleet of three ships, the island sheltered 3,000 pirates and more than 200 pirate ships rode at anchor in the harbor. Though resourceful and brave, Rogers clearly had no idea of the magnitude of the job facing him.

Captain Jennings, the founder of the settlement and a sort of elder statesman, advocated treating the new governor with kindness and pretending, for the time being, to accept the king's offer of clemency. He argued that Rogers could in time be corrupted as had most other officials sent by London. Most of the pirates agreed with Jennings on this plan of action. There was, however, one dissenting vote, and the man behind it was determined to have his way. A captain named Charlie Vane had just returned from a short cruise with a mouth-watering prize: a French brigantine loaded with sugar, brandy, and wine. Vane was concerned about Rogers' approach and feared that Jennings' plan would require him to surrender his rich prize. His idea was to fight, using both the fort at the harbor's mouth and the pirate fleet in the harbor, to drive Rogers off in fear of his life. Jennings held firm saying this would be only a temporary solution to a long-term problem. He stuck by his plan to kill Rogers with kindness until such time as the pirates could lure him over to their side.

Pirates attacking a merchant ship. Gilbert (Giraudon/Art Resource, N.Y.)

Vane was livid. It is said it took many glasses of rum to calm him down. He expected — indeed demanded — that the whole community pitch in and fight for his right to keep his loot. Jennings said it was unrealistic to fight and jeopardize the safety of all the pirates and the future of New Providence as the perfect base of operations. Vane screamed that he would be damned if he would surrender.

By now Rogers' three warships were blocking the harbor's entrances. Vane's compromise, he told Jennings, was to send a note to Rogers saying he would surrender if, and only if, he might keep his ill-gotten gains. The note he sent to Rogers is at once a masterpiece of pirate charm and chicanery. It reads:

To His Excellency The Governor of New Providence

Your Excellency may please to understand that we are willing to accept His Majesty's most gracious pardon on the following terms, viz.

That you will suffer us to dispose of all our goods now in our possession. Likewise to act as we see fit with everything belonging to us, as His Majesty's Act of Grace specifies. If Your Excellency shall please to comply with this we shall with all readiness accept of His Majesty's Act of Grace. If not, we are obliged to stand on our defense.

    So conclude
    Your humble servants

    Charles Vane and company

P.S. We wait a speedy answer.

Rogers knew full well the king's proclamation said nothing of the sort either in fact or intent. He would not dignify this message with an answer. Just after nightfall, with the harbor blockaded by Rogers' three ships, the action began.

Having transferred as much of the loot as possible from the captured French ship to his own, Vane and his crew attempted to make a run for it and put to sea. As a diversion, and a clever one at that, Vane had pointed the French brigantine directly at one of Rogers' ships and set it under way. She sailed straight for the blockading vessel. The catch was that directly prior to cutting her loose Vane had set the ship on fire. Imagine the English sailors as they watched an unmanned, burning ship sailing at a good clip directly for them. There was no room in the channel for the English ship to maneuver their big vessel out of the way of the burning ship, and all they could do was to run for the open sea. Eventually the fire reached the powder magazines and the French ship erupted into a massive fire ball accompanied by deafening noise as all the ship's guns fired randomly.

Under the light provided by the fire, Rogers watched as Charlie Vane's sloop slinked out of the channel. He had succeeded in keeping his loot and embarrassing the newly arrived governor. The pirates watching from the island were delighted. Not only were they genuinely happy for Vane, but they also rejoiced at the thought that Rogers was just another stooge sent out by London to do an impossible job.

But the pirates had severely underestimated the measure of their opponent. Rogers was not like any other governor, and he meant business. A revolutionary new era was about to begin.

Woodes Rogers

In 1718, when Woodes Rogers was commissioned to clean up New Providence and send the pirates packing, he already enjoyed notoriety as one of England's greatest captain adventurers. Just ten years prior he had been a virtually unknown Bristol merchant. During the War of the Spanish Succession he became frustrated when he lost many of his ships to Spanish and French privateers, and he vowed to avenge himself. Together with a few other Bristol merchants he outfitted two warships, christened them the *Duke* and the *Duchess*, and went hunting for Spaniards and Frenchmen. He took along plenty of supplies, a formidable armament of guns and ammunition, and his pet bulldog. Ironically, his conduct as a privateer was not so different from that of the pirates whose enemy he was later to become. Three years later he returned to Bristol rich and famous.

Rogers and his crew captured several Spanish and French privateers and in the process circumnavigated the globe, which only served to increase his renown. In 1711 only a handful of men had accomplished this feat. Rogers had the distinction of capturing what was reportedly one of the richest prizes ever taken. It was a Spanish plate galleon carrying silver worth £800,000, enough for Rogers and his entire crew to retire comfortably for the rest of their lives. Rogers, however, paid dearly for this fortune. During the battle to take the Spanish treasure ship, he was struck in the mouth by a musket ball. It shattered his jaw, disfiguring him for life.

If Rogers had done nothing else, his name would still be remembered by history for one chance deed. While cruising the Juan Fernández Islands, off the coast of Chile, Rogers rescued a Scot who had been marooned there for some time. The man's name was Alexander Selkirk, and he achieved immortality when Daniel Defoe told his story in *Robinson Crusoe*.

In a single voyage, lasting three years, Rogers accumulated great wealth and fame. It was the ideal to which every privateer aspired. He was not a greedy man and was content to return to his old life, rather than chase around the world in search of more wealth and adventure.

By 1717, however, Rogers had again begun to lose patience with brigandage on the high seas. The New Providence pirates were regularly stealing his ships. They were becoming more costly and troublesome to him than the Spanish and French had been. Rogers complained loudly to the Crown that the pirates should be suppressed. The government was so impressed with his vehemence that they enlisted him for the job. The lofty title bestowed upon him was "Captain General and Governor in Chief in and over the Bahamas in America." He was requested by His Majesty George I to bring about the peaceful colonization of the islands and to that end was granted the right to collect taxes and royalties from the inhabitants of the islands, if he could.

These were the circumstances under which Rogers found himself confronting the massed strength of the pirates of New Providence.

The morning after Rogers's close encounter with Charlie Vane he stood on the deck of his ship and looked out at the island. Although he knew that he might be walking into a trap, he made preparations to go ashore. As he approached the island, he found the pirates, in a more or less orderly fashion, lined up waiting for him. All were heavily armed, each with at least a cutlass and pistol, and some had muskets slung over their shoulders. Rogers must have passed some anxious moments until one of the pirates spoke up and read a prepared speech welcoming the new governor and stating that the entire population of New Providence was ready to accept His Majesty's pardon.

Rogers spoke to the crowd explaining his mission in New Providence. It was, he said, twofold: first, to reestablish colonial government in the Bahamas; second, to represent His Majesty in granting pardon to all who were ready to accept it and give up their life of piracy. He announced that he was ready then and there to accept the pledge of anyone who wanted to receive His Majesty's Grace. At this, Captain Jennings, the island's elder statesman, turned to the crowd of pirates and bellowed, "All right, you bastards, line up!" Captain Jennings had orchestrated a plan to lull Rogers into a false sense of security. Toward this end, Jennings loudly paid his respects to the new governor, announcing that he forswore all acts of piracy, now and forever, so help him God! Hundreds of pirates fol-

OVERLEAF — William Hogarth's portrait of 1729 shows Rogers, now governor of New Providence, with his family. The globe at his right is a reminder of Rogers's successful circumnavigation (National Maritime Museum, London).

lowed his example. Watching this spectacle and still recovering from his astonishment, Governor Rogers might well have wondered at the pirates' new-found good intentions.

For the first few weeks on the island Rogers enjoyed an uneasy truce with the pirates. It was a tense time for Rogers because he knew that very soon the two warships that had escorted him would have to sail off to their next assignment. Rogers declared martial law on the island and kept a close watch over all comings and goings.

Soon after Rogers was approached by a pirate captain who congratulated him for putting on a brave show. The officials in London, he said, had every reason to be satisfied. Now, perhaps, they could get down to business. He offered Rogers a percentage of all plunder and could not believe it when Rogers had him physically removed from his office, threatening to have him arrested for attempted bribery.

With the failure of this early attempt to buy off the governor, the pirates began questioning Jennings' plan. Some were in favor of an uprising. Jennings once again stepped in and persuaded everyone to wait a while longer.

In the meantime Rogers had been doing some planning of his own. His first step was an early attempt at land reform. He offered acreage to any man who would promise an honest attempt to improve and cultivate it. Next, he informed the pirate population that the Spanish were planning an attack on the island. The only thing the pirates hated more than the representatives of English law and order were the Spaniards. The early history of the New World was one long succession of battles between Englishmen and Spaniards, with each side accusing the other of the most heinous acts.

Now the pirates had a new reason to fight; New Providence was legally their own. They had official deeds to their plots and were called on to defend them against the Spanish Papists. They were now acting as established landowners protecting their homes from an invader. It was at this point that Captain Vane returned to the scene and helped Rogers in a way neither he, Rogers, nor anyone else could have possibly foreseen or imagined. Vane, having joined forces with the infamous Stede Bonnet, had returned to New Providence threatening to take the island by force. Rogers seized this opportunity to rally the pirates' new found pride in their island home.

In a meeting with Captain Jennings and Captain Benjamin Hornigold, a founding father of piracy in the New World and mentor of the infamous Blackbeard, Rogers set forth their tactical position. As governor of the island, Rogers was gravely concerned that Vane and Bonnet could, with some effort, knock out the guns of the island's fortress, dangerously weaken its defenses and make it possible for the Spaniards to take the island. Exercising no small amount of duplicity, Rogers said all was not yet lost. There were some English warships in the vicinity and perhaps they might

Portrait of Daniel Defoe by Michiel van der Guicht. In addition to his fame as the creator of Robinson Crusoe, Defoe has been credited by some scholars as being the true author of Johnson's *A General History of Pirates* (National Portrait Gallery, London).

This engraving shows Rogers in 1709 at an early stage in his career checking Spanish ladies in Guayaquil, Ecuador, for gold and silver. Artist unknown (Hulton Getty Picture Collection).

engage and either chase away or destroy Vane and Bonnet. After all, a ship is the only way to catch a ship. Captain Hornigold, after draining his mug of rum, suggested that maybe a couple of pirate ships could do the job. Jennings agreed and the two volunteered for the job. They even went so far as to propose that Rogers commission them as privateers, legally entitling them to hunt down (they paused for a moment before daring to utter the next word), pirates!

So it came to pass that Rogers accomplished one of history's oddest, and most significant, feats. Captain Hornigold, a pirate through and through, set out with two armed ships to hunt down and capture his old compatriots. This marked a turning point in the history of New Providence, and in a sense, in the history of piracy as well. With one bold stroke Rogers almost entirely ended its unchallenged dominion over the seas in the New World. From then on piracy in the Americas was on the decline. The Caribbean, where pirates had roamed free and imposed a reign of terror, now became unsafe and unfriendly to them. The impregnable pirate kingdom at New Providence was well on its way to becoming a law-abiding colony of the Crown.

Hornigold chased Vane all the way to Long Island Sound, but he never did succeed in his mission. During the chase Bonnet disappeared.

Back at New Providence Rogers commissioned all the pirates as privateers with the strict condition that they restrict themselves to attacking Spanish shipping. Although Spain and England were not presently at war, a constant state of warlike rivalry existed between the Spanish and English colonies.

Once again the event that cemented the governor's authority over the island was one he could not have planned on but which, once it occurred, he used to his full advantage. He had sent three ships to other islands to trade for badly needed provisions. The crews mutinied and voted to revert to piracy. Once again Rogers turned to Hornigold. This time Hornigold successfully captured the mutineers. Rogers set up a vice-admiralty court to try the prisoners. The court was presided over by Rogers and reformed pirates. The mutineers were found guilty by their former colleagues and hanged to death.

In 1719 the long-threatened war between Spain and England was finally, officially declared. Rogers prepared the island, his pirate militia, and a small fleet for the impending assault. It came in February 1720. The Spanish attacked with an overwhelming force of both ships and soldiers. The pirate fleet was easily overrun by the five men-of-war, three brigantines, and three sloops of the Spanish. The Spaniards poured onto the beaches and although they greatly outnumbered the defenders, amazingly the pirates stood fast and repelled them. New Providence was successfully defended, a testament to Woodes Rogers and his hold over the once lawless mob of pirates. With a remarkable display of resourcefulness, Rogers turned a pirate stronghold into a law-abiding community that then fought off a vastly superior force

The government at home in Great Britain showed no appreciation. Eventually Rogers' frustration caused him to resign his position and return to England. After seven years there he asked for and was restored to his position as governor of the Bahamas. His return to New Providence met with a joyful reception.

By the time he returned, the war with Spain had ended, as had any piracy operating from New Providence. Rogers devoted the rest of his life to attempting to turn the Bahamas into a planter's colony. He died in 1732 in office. His reformed pirates buried him with ceremony on a hill overlooking the beautiful blue-green waters of the Bahamas and the lucrative, peaceful settlement that was his legacy to the New World.

WILLIAM DAMPIER

William Dampier was a true adventurer. In the late seventeenth century he served on a number of buccaneer vessels and worked for a time in the notorious log-cutting camps of Mexico and Honduras.

During his career at sea, which spanned over thirty years, he circumnavigated the globe three times, the last as navigator to Woodes Rogers. He was, however, never very adept as a pirate. When he finally got to command his own vessel, it sank. Fortunately he and his crew were rescued by a passing ship.

Dampier's real fame is due to his writing. He published three invaluable accounts of his travels. The first, *A New Voyage around the World*, was a huge success. In addition to recounting his adventures in exotic places, his books benefited from the meticulous notes he kept on flora and fauna and provided valuable information about what were largely uncharted waters.

Though never very good with money, Dampier earned a full share of the booty captured by Rogers on his trip around the world and with that managed to end his days in relative comfort.

Portrait by Thomas Murray (National Portrait Gallery, London).

93

Contemporary engraving of Charlie Vane. (Library of Congress)

Charlie Vane

Charlie Vane was the personification of the successful, self-made pirate. Because of the tremendous victory Woodes Rogers achieved in subduing thousands of pirates, his distinction is more pronounced as he was the only person to openly and successfully defy the renowned governor. Vane's famous dash to the sea has, however, obscured his more significant accomplishments.

Becoming captain of a pirate ship was no easy task. It usually depended on ability and cunning. To become a captain, a pirate not only had to prove himself tougher and more daring than some very tough and daring pirates, but he also had to be elected captain by the crew. The life expectancy of a pirate captain was comparatively short. The percentage of pirate captains who perished at sea was far greater than that of the pirate hands.

Vane's first reported action clearly demonstrated his talents. Early in the eighteenth century, a Spanish galleon with a cargo of rich silver plate ran onto a reef and sank in the waters off Florida. Quickly sailing to the half-submerged treasure, like sharks drawn to blood, hundreds of pirates converged to dive for the silver. The cargo was so valuable that Spain dispatched two warships to drive off the scavengers while a Spanish ship hauled up the treasure. Once the pirates were driven off, the warships sailed on to attend to Spain's many other interests in the region. Then Vane struck. He wisely had chosen not to waste time, energy, or blood on a battle around the wreck or in the work of hauling. Once the silver was aboard the rescuing Spanish vessel, he attacked and took what turned out to be one of the richest prizes recorded in the history of piracy.

Shortly after escaping from Woodes Rogers on New Providence, Vane captured a Barbados sloop, which he kept, with its prize crew, and an island trader carrying a sizable quantity of pieces of eight. He kept this ship as well. The little fleet headed north, and all along the way ships seemed to fall right into their bloodthirsty hands. Among the prizes Vane took, while, it is worth mentioning, he was supposed to have been fleeing pursuit by Rogers' ships, were a merchantman from Ipswich, Massachusetts, another Barbados sloop, a sloop from Curaçao and a large brigantine from Africa loaded with ninety slaves.

Typically, pirates took great pleasure in capturing a slaver, torturing and killing the ship's captain and crew, and turning the slaves loose ashore. This time, however, Vane's plans to do just this were upset by trouble in the ranks of his little fleet. Vane had appointed a master by the name of Yeats to rule over the prize crew on board the captured Barbados sloop. Yeats did not openly defy Vane but rather incited the crew to mutiny. One night when the pirate fleet had anchored offshore of what is now Paris Island, the famous Marine training station, Yeats and his crew made a run for it. They had lost confidence in Vane and feared he was leading them to their ruin. They knew the king's pardon was still valid if they wanted to ask for it. Since they were very close to Charleston (then Charles Towne), they sent a message to the governor of South Carolina offering to surrender and take the pardon. The offer was accepted, and Yeats surrendered the sloop and all its cargo. This was tremendously unlucky for the ninety slaves from Africa who would have been set free if Vane had retained control of the vessel on which they sailed. The captain of the slaver was still aboard. He once again took charge of them and delivered them to the slave market for which they were originally intended. Vane, very angry over the loss of his prize, and perhaps even more upset with Yeats' treachery, nevertheless licked his wounds, put his sails to the wind, and headed north.

By a kind of serendipity Vane encountered Blackbeard and his crew having a drinking party at their base in Ocracoke Inlet in the colony of North Carolina. Vane and company joined in the revelry. The drinking party started in mid-September 1718, and it was early October before anyone was sober enough to handle sails and helm and ride the tide out to sea.

While recovering from what must have been a fierce hangover, Vane's crew sailed north to Long Island. Here they captured a brigantine and a sloop, looted them and sent them on their way. Then Vane headed south again and only by good fortune didn't cross paths with Ben Hornigold. Apparently, he did not know that his old colleague, now in the service of Governor Woodes Rogers, was hunting for him.

As Vane sailed along the New Jersey coast he encountered what seemed a fairly easy prize waiting to be taken. Vane felt certain that the simple act of hoisting the black flag would be enough to frighten the ship into surrender. To his great surprise, not only did she not surrender, but she fired a thundering broadside and raised the colors of a French man-of-war.

Vane was a hard-headed businessman. He could be brave when necessary, as he had demonstrated many times. But he knew the difference between bravery and madness, and this looked like madness. He decided

"Pirates Used to Do That to Their Captains Now and Then." Howard Pyle's illustration shows how tenuous a pirate captain's hold over his crew could be.

to stand down and make haste. Members of his crew disagreed with his decision. Vane called their attention to the ship's articles of all pirate vessels, which stated that in time of imminent enemy action the captain and only the captain was in full command.

However, the same articles specified that once the danger is past the rest of the crew could vote to depose the captain if they wished. The hot-blooded young ship's quartermaster, John Rackham, forced the issue and incited the crew to call for this vote of confidence. Rackham, later to become known as "Calico Jack," was to earn a place in pirate history for a far different reason than his service under Charlie Vane. To his own astonishment, Vane lost the vote of confidence and he, together with those who had remained loyal to him, were unceremoniously put onto one of the prize sloops to be sent away.

As Vane watched the pirate fleet sail away, he realized he had come full circle. From the lowly status of indigent sailor he had achieved fame

EXECUTION of the PIRATES

'Whoso sheddeth man's blood, by man shall his blood be shed.'

Particulars of the Murder perpetrated by the Pirates for which th.. ..re this day to suffer public Execution---Sketch of their LIVES, and of their behavior since the awful sentence of Death was passed upon them.

Broadside. Execution of Pirates. (Peabody Essex Museum, Salem Mass.).

98

and wealth as the captain of an entire fleet. Now he stood aboard a small, unarmed sloop with a small desperate crew at the mercy of both their pursuers and the elements.

Lesser men might have become disheartened by this bad luck, but Charlie Vane was made of tougher stuff. He armed his sloop and within three days had attacked and captured three other small vessels. Three months later Vane could boast of a fleet of four ships, larger than his previous command. He had not only recovered from his reverses but had surpassed his earlier successes. But then, while cruising in the Bay of Honduras, a terrible and sudden hurricane struck. The ships were separated and Vane's sloop was run aground. All hands were lost with the exception of Vane himself.

Vane was stranded on a tiny island. No money, tattered clothing, and most importantly no visible means of escape. He survived on fish and bananas. After some time a big Jamaican sloop drifted into the harbor. Vane was overjoyed when it turned out that the ship's captain was an ex-pirate and old friend named Holiford. One can only try to imagine Vane's horror when Holiford refused to take him aboard. Holiford said, "Charles, I shan't trust you aboard my ship; unless I carry you a prisoner, I shall have you caballing with my men, knock me on the head and run away with my ship apirating." Even Vane, a master of chicanery, must have had a hard time finding a reply.

Not long after Holiford's departure, another large ship put into the island's harbor. This ship's captain, having no knowledge of Charles Vane, took the stranded man aboard as a new hand. Vane was already making plans when a strange and highly unlikely event occurred. The vessel that had just taken Vane aboard sighted another sail heading toward them. The second ship was none other than the Jamaican commanded by Holiford. As it turned out, Holiford and Vane's new captain were old friends. Holiford came aboard for dinner, sighted Vane and sealed his fate. Waiting until he was alone with Vane's new captain, Holiford informed him of the true identity of his new deckhand. Holiford offered to take him aboard and surrender him at Jamaica. They agreed on this course of action. Minutes later, Vane was aboard Holiford's ship, clamped in irons. A few days later his old friend, now a reformed pirate, handed him over to the authorities at Port Royal. Within the week Captain Charles Vane, the self-made pirate who had twice risen above the odds, was hanged by the neck until dead.

Pyle's animated depiction of Kidd on board the *Adventure Galley*.

Captain Kidd

No name conjures up more vividly the romantic image of the bloodthirsty pirate than that of Captain William Kidd. The reality was, however, considerably different.

Generations of fiction writers have created a mythical Captain Kidd. Even Robert Louis Stevenson refers to Kidd in his famous work *Treasure Island*. In fiction Kidd is always portrayed as bold and dashing, ruthlessly commanding his crew while terrorizing the seven seas. In point of fact, Kidd was a pirate of mediocre caliber and in the end an unlucky villain. As Philip Gosse commented, "if Kidd's reputation was in just proportion to his actual deeds, he would have been forgotten as soon as he had been 'turned off' at Wapping Old Stairs." Kidd made a single voyage during which he captured only one significant prize. Other pirates were far crueler, took more booty, and roamed the seas far longer than did Kidd.

What then is the reason for Kidd's lasting notoriety? It may have been due to his terrible fate at the hands of a corrupt establishment. His trial incriminated royal officials and caused a political scandal. Or it may be attributable to the mysterious process by which legends grow and are passed down from one generation to the next. Though he took only one substantial ship, Kidd's story is fascinating as much for the behind-the-scenes intrigue as for his actual acts of piracy.

Not much is known for certain about Kidd's early life. In 1689 he served on the pirate ship *Blessed William*, which surrendered to the British in the same year at the Caribbean island of Nevis. During the Nine Years' War (1688–97) the British and French used buccaneers to loot the other side's colonies. The British governor of Nevis licensed the *Blessed William as* a privateer and Kidd became its captain.

In December 1689 Kidd joined a squadron that battled French ships. Deciding that piracy was less risky than war, the *Blessed William*'s crew stole the ship in February 1690 while Kidd was ashore. Kidd was given a

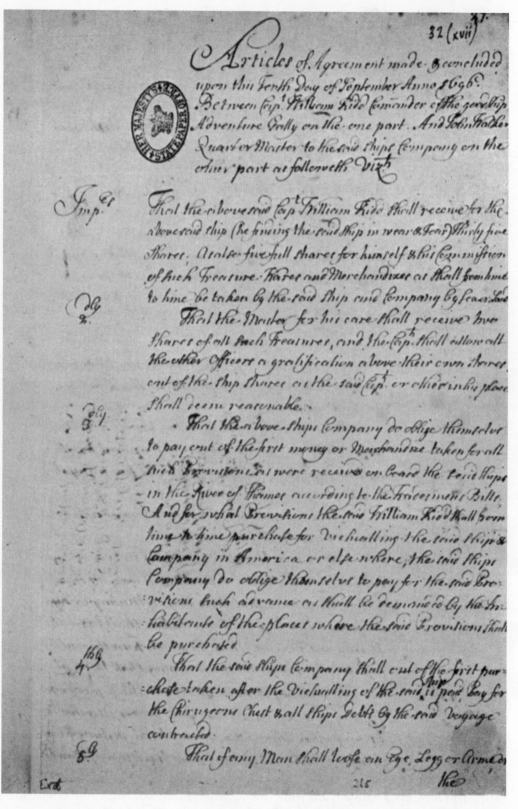

Part of the articles drawn up between Captain Kidd and his crew. Colonial
Office Papers (C.O. 5/861)

ship named the *Antigua* with which he chased the *Blessed William* to New York, but he arrived in New York too late to catch her. He decided to try life on land for while and in May 1691 married Sarah Oort, a wealthy widow. Although in her early twenties, Oort had already outlived two husbands. For the next few years he cultivated local political leaders, becoming a confidant of Colonel Benjamin Fletcher, the governor of New York.

Kidd quickly amassed a fortune and acquired expensive waterfront property in lower Manhattan. He was an active member of his community. He purchased a pew at Trinity Episcopal Church and had many friends in the congregation. Among his contacts was Robert Livingston, an ambitious entrepreneur.

In 1695 Kidd sailed the *Antigua* to London, hoping to get a privateering license from the Admiralty Court. In London he and Livingston met with Richard Coote, Earl of Bellomont, an Irish peer recently nominated as royal governor of New York and Massachusetts. The three men conceived a scheme to capture pirates and keep their booty, instead of returning it to its original owners.

Kidd, Bellomont, and Livingston signed a contract. Kidd was made captain and Bellomont put up £6,000, four-fifths of the cost. Through separate secret agreements, Bellomont split his shares with four high-ranking partners — including the secretary of state and the heads of the Admiralty and the judiciary. These sponsors were to keep the lion's share of the loot, although King William III was promised ten percent of the value of all captured goods and money.

In return for his ten percent, the king granted three commissions. A standard privateering letter permitted Kidd to capture French merchant shipping. Under a special royal decree Kidd was authorized to arrest pirates anywhere in the world. A third letter allowed Kidd to keep captured booty without going through the courts. To prevent him from cheating his partners he was ordered to surrender his loot to Governor Coote in Boston. In retrospect it seems bizarre that the man who was to become one of the most famous outlaws of the sea originally set sail with a license to arrest pirates.

Kidd himself apparently had apprehensions and misgivings about the practicality of the arrangement. He understood as well as anyone the fine distinction between privateering and piracy. He knew that it was common practice for privateer crews to turn pirate if disappointed by a lack of plunder. But he was afraid of being branded disloyal by refusing a royal commission. In addition, Kidd feared a refusal would ruin his other chances for economic advancement. As he later said, "I thinking myself safe with a King's commission and the protection of so many great men accepted thinking it was in my Lord Bellomont's power as Governor of

New York, to oppress me if I still continued obstinate. Before I went to sea I waited twice on my Lord Romney and Admiral Russell [two of the secret partners]. Both hastened me to sea, and promised to stand by me."

The partners bought the *Adventure Galley*, a 300 ton, 34-gun vessel that carried 23 pairs of oars for maneuvering when becalmed. Kidd left England in May 1696 with the *Adventure Galley* and approximately 70 men. He returned to New York where he intended to recruit the remaining 80 hands needed for a full ship's complement. The only way Kidd could hope to attract a capable crew was to promise them 60 percent of any booty — even though he already had pledged 60 percent to Bellomont and his partners. Great care and attention was directed to the task of securing a reliable crew, men who would not, when confronted with pirates, become pirates themselves. In spite of this effort, the 150 men eventually selected were of questionable backgrounds. Governor Fletcher after reviewing the crew referred to them as "men of desperate fortunes and necessities, in expectation of getting vast treasure. It is generally believed here that if he misses the design named in his commission, he will not be able to govern such a villainous herd."

After six months under sail along the African coast and into the Indian Ocean with no prize to show for their labors, the crew recruited in New York began to openly advocate piracy. They bitterly resented Kidd's failure to find any plunder thus far. No one knows if it was due to the pressure from his crew or his own desire, but it was at this point that Kidd and the *Adventure Galley* turned decidedly pirate. Had he wanted to honor his license, he could have attacked John Hoar, Dirk Chivers, and other pirates at nearby Saint Mary's Island, the tiny, lawless outpost off the coast of Madagascar. He instead sailed for the Red Sea to plunder the pilgrim fleets returning from Mecca to India.

On August 15, 1697, the *Adventure Galley* caught up with an Indian squadron accompanied by an East India Company ship. When the British vessel fired at the *Galley*, Kidd retreated toward northwestern India. On August 19 he captured a small vessel near Janjira, tortured the Indian sailors, and took food and some money. The British captain was forced into labor for several months as the pilot of the *Galley*.

In September the *Galley* fought off two Portuguese warships and visited the Laccadive Islands, off India's west coast, for repairs. Kidd's men forced the islanders to work for free and raped several women. In November they came across a Dutch vessel. William Moore, the *Adventure Galley* gunner may have wanted to attack and during a violent argument Kidd smashed a bucket on Moore's head, killing him.

Kidd took two more prizes off the Indian coast. At the end of November he seized the *Rouparelle*. Although Dutch-owned, the *Rouparelle* flew the French flag and her papers included a French "pass" (passport). Off Cochin on January 12, 1698, Kidd took the only truly rich prize of his

Nineteenth century engraving by an unknown artist shows Kidd committing the crime that would send him to the gallows.

career. The *Quedah Merchant* was leased to officials of the Indian government but carried a French pass. Kidd kept the *Merchant* and her crew and sold some of her cargo of cloth. Continuing south he seized a small Portuguese vessel and unsuccessfully pursued the *Dorrill* and the *Sedgwick*, two East India Company ships.

In April 1698 the *Adventure Galley* landed at Saint Mary's Island, where Robert Culliford's *Mocha* was already moored. Since Culliford had helped steal Kidd's ship in 1690, both men were initially suspicious of each other. But Kidd quickly reassured the pirates that he had reformed and that now "he was as bad as they."

The booty was divided when the *Quedah Merchant* arrived flying the Jolly Roger and captained by a deputy appointed by Kidd. Under the ship's articles Kidd kept 40 shares, somewhat less than 40 percent of the take. Most of Kidd's crew enlisted with Culliford, who sailed from Saint Mary's in June 1698. In November Kidd burned the rotted-out *Adventure Galley* and departed in the *Quedah Merchant*, renamed the *Adventure Prize*.

Kidd's capture of the *Quedah Merchant* threatened the East India Company. Already enraged by Henry Every's sack of the *Gunsway* in 1695, the Indian emperor threatened to expel all European traders. Under pressure, the company compensated the owners for goods on the *Merchant*, paid large bribes, and agreed to patrol the South Indian Sea. But Indian officials continued to blame the company for new pirate attacks.

To answer Indian complaints, British officials had to punish Kidd's crimes. He was branded a pirate and omitted by name from a general pardon issued in 1698. In November 1698 the government ordered its colonial governors to conduct an all-out manhunt. Kidd learned that he was a wanted man when the *Adventure Prize* reached the Caribbean island of Anguilla in April 1699. After the Danish governor of St. Thomas refused his protection, Kidd went to Mona Island and Savona Bay in Hispaniola. British traders bought cloth from the pirate, and one sold Kidd a sloop. The *Prize* was looted and burned after he left.

With stops at New Jersey and Long Island, Kidd headed for Boston. Kidd trusted he would receive fair treatment from Bellomont, and for good reason. Bellomont had written to Kidd saying, "I have advised with His Majesty's Council and shewed them this letter and they are of the opinion, that if you can be so clear as you have said, then you may safely come hither. And I make no manner of doubt but to obtain the King's pardon for you, and for those few men you have left who I understand, have been faithful to you, and refused as well as you to dishonour the Commission you have from England. I assure you on my word and honor, I will perform nicely what I have promised." At the same time, Bellomont confided in a letter to London: "Menacing him had not been the way to invite him hither, but rather wheedling." Immediately upon his arrival in July 1699 Bellomont arrested him, sending him under armed guard to London, where he arrived in April 1700.

OPPPOSITE — Kidd burying his treasure at Gardiners Island. Howard Pyle. Though the precise whereabouts of Kidd's hoard have never been established, anecdotal evidence supports Pyle's choice of Gardiners Island.

OVERLEAF — Captain William Kidd hung in chains at Tilbury as an example for passing sailors, 1701. William Gilkerson (By kind permission of the artist).

His case became embroiled in British politics. The opposition party in the British Parliament tried to impeach the sponsors of his voyage, and Kidd testified before the House of Commons in March 1701. The impeachment vote narrowly failed, but Kidd's presence was an embarrassment to powerful people. Only his execution would remove him as a potentially dangerous witness.

In May 1701 Kidd was convicted of murdering William Moore and robbing the *Quedah Merchant* and other ships. He argued that the *Rouparelle* and *Merchant* had been legal prizes because they sailed under French passes. (The war between England and France had ended, but the peace treaty applied south of the equator only after March 1698.) Kidd had given the passes to Bellomont for safe-keeping, but Admiralty officials anxious to see Kidd convicted and executed, hid them during the trial.

Kidd was hanged at Wapping on May 23, 1701, and his body was hung in chains farther down the Thames as a warning to all who might be seduced by the promised riches of piracy. His legend has endured as have the rumors that he buried fabulous treasure somewhere between India and Boston.

Ballad of Captain Kidd

My name was William Kidd, when I sailed, when I sailed
My name was William Kidd, when I sailed
My name was William Kidd
God's law I did forbid,
And so wickedly I did, when I sailed

My parents taught me well, when I sailed, when I sailed
My parents taught me well, when I sailed
to shun the gates of hell
But 'gainst them I rebelled, when I sailed

I'd a Bible in my hand, when I sailed, when I sailed
I'd a Bible in my hand,
By my father's great command,
And sunk it in the sand, when I sailed

I murdered William Moore, as I sailed, as I sailed
I murdered William Moore, as I sailed
I murdered William Moore,
And laid him in his gore,
Not many leagues from shore, as I sailed

I was sick and nigh to death, when I sailed, when I sailed
I was sick and nigh to death, when I sailed
I was sick and nigh to death
And I vowed at every breath
To walk in wisdom's ways, as I sailed

I thought I was undone, as I sailed, as I sailed
I thought I was undone, as I sailed
And my wicked glass hath run,
But health did soon return, as I sailed

My repentance lasted not, as I sailed, as I sailed
My repentance lasted not, as I sailed
My repentance lasted not
My vows I soon forgot
Damnation was my lot, as I sailed

I spyed the ships from France, as I sailed, as I sailed
I spyed the ships of France, as I sailed
I spyed the ships from France
To them I did advance
And took them all by chance, as I sailed

I spyed the ships of Spain, as I sailed, as I sailed
I spyed the ships of Spain, as I sailed
I spyed the ships of Spain,
I fired on them amain,
Till most of them was slain, as I sailed

I'd ninety bars of gold, as I sailed, as I sailed
I'd ninety bars of gold, as I sailed
I'd ninety bars of gold,
And dollars manifold,
With riches uncontrolled, as I sailed

Thus being o'ertaken at last, I must die, I must die
Thus being o'ertaken at last, I must die
Thus being o'ertaken at last,
And into prison cast,
And sentence being past, I must die

Farewell, the raging main, I must die, I must die
Farewell, the raging main, I must die
Farewell, the raging main
To Turkey, France and Spain
I shall n'er see you again, I must die

To Execution Dock, I must go, I must go
To Execution Dock, I must go
To Execution Dock,
Will many thousands flock,
But I must bear the shock, and must die

Nineteenth century engraving shows Kidd kicking the family Bible

Come all ye young and old, see me die, see me die
Come all ye young and old, see me die
Come all ye young and old,
You're welcome to my gold,
For by it I've lost my soul, and must die

Take warning now by me, for I must die, for I must die
Take warning now by me, for I must die
Take warning now by me,
And shun bad company,
Lest you come to hell with me, for I die

Contemporary engraving of Edward England (Library of Congress).

Edward England

Rife with contradictions, the life of Edward England was as full of vicissitudes as it was short-lived. Edward England was an Irishman and a pirate, who, it has been said, was guilty of having too much compassion. Soft-hearted pirates were not usually very successful. He was good-natured, but for that very reason had trouble controlling his crew. Captain Johnson described him as "having a great deal of good nature . . . courageous, not over-avaricious, humane, but too often overruled."

England began his pirate career when, as an officer of a Jamaican sloop, he was captured by the pirate Captain Christopher Winter. England joined his band, which, like so many others, was based at New Providence Island. When Woodes Rogers subdued the island, England made off and took several prizes along the African coast as well as in the Azores and Cape Verde Islands.

In one action England took a large ship and, after renaming it the *Pearl*, used it rather than his sloop as his own ship. He joined forces with John Taylor, after capturing a prize commanded by the latter. England and Taylor looted several vessels along the Malabar coast of India, where England exchanged the *Pearl* for the 34-gun *Fancy*.

Their next stop was Madagascar, a pirate haunt second only to New Providence in popularity among pirate captains. In the Comoros harbor of Johanna Island they found three large ships of the East Indies trade, two English and one Dutch. Two of the ships ran off upon spotting the pirates, but one was heavily armed, the *Cassandra* commanded by Captain James Macrae. The *Fancy* and the *Cassandra* squared off in a bloody battle firing one broadside after another. The fighting lasted several hours with both ships' crews fighting fiercely and bravely. Finally, Macrae realized that he was going to lose the battle. Together with most of his crew he successfully escaped ashore. Aboard the *Cassandra*, England's boarding party found cargo worth nearly £75,000, a veritable fortune for the

England's mild temperament led to his being deposed and abandoned by the crew of the Cassandra. From Johnson's *A General History of Pirates*.

time. The *Cassandra* suffered 37 casualties and more than 90 pirates were killed in the action.

Macrae hid for ten days and then took a daring chance. Hoping to find a victorious pirate captain whose greed for treasure and thirst for blood had by now been satiated, Macrae decided to go aboard the *Fancy* and ask for mercy. Also, being somewhat familiar with pirate customs, Macrae hoped to find England made magnanimous from the liquor he would have doubtlessly consumed in celebration of his victory.

Some wanted Macrae put to death immediately, but others, who had served under him, had tremendous respect for him. England and Taylor argued bitterly over Macrae's fate until finally Taylor, softened up by rum punch, deferred to England's desire to act with leniency and grant Macrae his life.

Macrae survived and was rewarded handsomely by the East India Company for meritorious service and extreme bravery. England, on the other hand, did not fare quite as well. Because of his clemency to Macrae, his crew turned against him. He was removed as captain and marooned with the three crewmen who supported him on Mauritius, an islet near Madagascar. (One of England's companions who was described in Captain Johnson's *General History* as " a man with a terrible pair of whiskers and a wooden leg, being stuck round with pistols," became Robert Louis Stevenson's model for the character of Long John Silver in *Treasure Island*.)

The four men sailed to Madagascar in a tiny unseaworthy boat, somehow arriving safely at their destination. England never rebounded from this setback. With no money, he was reduced to begging and accepting the charity of others. No one knows if it was due to extreme disillusionment or a loss of the will to keep going, but England died not long after his arrival at Madagascar.

Blackbeard

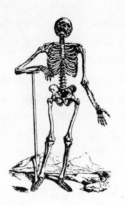

The name Edward Teach probably means very little or nothing at all to most people. The name Blackbeard, however, is instantly familiar. Blackbeard's real name has been said to have been Teach or Thatch or Tache (no one seems to know for sure). What is certain is that Blackbeard migrated to the West Indies from his native Bristol, England where he had been a starving ragamuffin of an orphan. At the time half the population of England lived in poverty, and for a poor, young boy to survive took a great deal of determination and an enterprising spirit. Young Edward Teach had both qualities in abundance. He found a berth on a merchantman and made his way to New Providence, where he crossed paths with Ben Hornigold.

The mean streets of Bristol had schooled him well; they had hardened his character and left him with a brooding desire for revenge. From the beginning, as an eager young hand aboard Hornigold's ship, Teach displayed a gift for marksmanship, a talent for dirty, close-at-hand work, and a thirst for blood unmatched by any pirate of his time. Hornigold was quick to recognize these "attributes" and made the young Teach his protégé.

After his "apprenticeship" with Captain Hornigold, Teach went out on his own. Within a few months he had become the most feared and despised pirate in the Americas. There was not a merchant skipper on the Spanish Main who did not go cold at the mention of his name.

OPPOSITE — Blackbeard with burning matches in his hair. From Johnson's *A General History of Pirates.*

His repulsiveness was part genuine and part affectation. He took his name from the spectacular beard he had grown, a matted greasy mess of jet-black hair, that covered nearly his entire face and hung down to his chest. He was as dirty as he was hairy. The mixture of smells — liquor, sweat, and swill made it physically challenging to remain for long in his presence. His coat and pants were typically streaked with food, slime, and blood. His enormous hands were caked with the dirt and grime of many voyages. His countenance was fearsome, marked by a pair of over-sized mutilated ears, bulging red-veined eyes, a twisted, broken nose, and raw, curling lips that blubbered when he was in his usual state of drunk-enness. His entire appearance, partly by design, partly by nature was cal-culated to strike fear in the heart of any honest citizen unfortunate enough to cross his path.

In action Blackbeard was a terrifying figure. Loaded down with pis-tols and cutlasses, he was a walking arsenal. He braided his beard. At the moment of boarding his prey, he stuck slow burning matches in his hair. Sailors are on the whole a superstitious group, and many, at the sight of Blackbeard's illuminated face, believed they were being attacked by the Devil himself. This is how it happened that time after time merchant ships that might otherwise have strongly resisted instead fell prize to Black-beard with scarcely a struggle. Blackbeard rarely killed his captives or even burned their ships. In fact, if everyone did exactly as ordered, loot-ing was the extent of the damage. But the slightest resistance moved Blackbeard to set an example. If a victim did not volunteer to remove a diamond ring, Blackbeard chopped it off, finger and all. This not only left its mark on the victim, but infected all those who heard the tale with ter-ror. Often the mere mention of the pirate's name was enough. The most important function of these tactics was to spread the word that, while Blackbeard could be merciful to those who cooperated, woe to those who did not. The success of this strategy exceeded Blackbeard's wildest expec-tations.

Within a few months of the time he had set out on his own in the *Queen Anne's Revenge*, he had become the most notorious pirate captain in the Americas.

Blackbeard had the highest regard for his own achievements. He looked down on other pirate captains. Aboard his ship he was a tyrant. His own men suffered under his heavy hand, but they never voted him down because he brought them so many rich prizes. Ashore, he was loud, belligerent, and perpetually drunk; but again his fellow pirate captains put up with him largely for fear of his well-deserved reputation for bar-baric cruelty.

OPPOSITE — Blackbeard interviewing a new recruit. Howard Pyle.

Shore leave for Blackbeard and his crew was more in the nature of an assault. It was said that dogs, cats, birds and other creatures credited with the gift of premonition fled the area at least an hour before the *Revenge* sailed into the harbor.

As drinking was the main attraction of shore leave, tavern keepers had much to lose or gain. One visit from Blackbeard could either make their fortune or ruin them, depending on the whim of the roaring drunkard leading the singing at the head of the center table. Blackbeard preferred taverns with serving girls. However, few taverns, especially on New Providence, employed women because there was more money to be earned in other occupations. This deficiency however, was usually made up for by the swarms of girls who would arrive at the tavern minutes after Blackbeard. A bystander might observe the divergent paths of males and females at the door to a tavern taken over by Blackbeard — the men would stagger out and run away as fast as they could, while the ladies of opportunity would pour in on their own form of treasure hunt. Crew members familiar with the drill were smart enough to leave the ship with only enough money for one night's revelry. The New Providence girls who were accomplished at their trade directed their attention to the newly arrived crews who were likely to drink harder and have more money to spend.

Legend has it that Blackbeard treated the girls with far more consideration than his crewmen did. Despite his cruelties, his contempt for his fellow men, his bluster, and his boorishness, he became heartsick with infatuation over every harbor-town girl who caught his fancy. Blackbeard is said to have become so involved with women while on shore leave that it was quite common for him to propose marriage by the time he was ready to board ship.

Blackbeard would carry his fiancé aboard the *Revenge* and the first mate, with the sort of disinterest that comes from performing a repetitive chore, would solemnly read the marriage service and pronounce them man and wife. It is doubtful that his "brides" deluded themselves into thinking they were truly married. However, even if the ceremony was little more than a gesture, it seems Blackbeard's "brides" did far better financially than those he took an interest in but never married. Among Blackbeard's crew his marriages were a source of great amusement. In spite of his repeated vows never to "marry" again, he is credited with having had fourteen wives before he died.

In the spring of 1717 Blackbeard sailed away from New Providence for the last time. (A few months later Woodes Rogers would begin his clean-up of this important seat of piratical activity). Blackbeard had

OPPOSITE — Blackbeard with pistol in hand. From Johnson's *A General History of Pirates*.

Portrait of Alexander Spotswood, governor of Virginia (1710–22). Charles Bridges (Virginia State Library, Richmond).

decided to switch his home base to the town of Bath (then Bath Towne) in North Carolina, feeling that it was a more congenial site for conducting his affairs. He made Ocracoke Inlet his base of operations. The governor of North Carolina, Charles Eden, had no scruples about doing business with pirates, especially as the potential profits were enormous. By this time the King's Act of Grace, the offer of a general pardon for piracy, had been proclaimed. Eden simply pardoned Blackbeard and his crew without bothering to relieve them of their plunder. Naturally there was no suggestion of reforming the pirate. Blackbeard accepted the pardon, sold his loot, then rested until it was time for another cruise.

On route to Bath, Blackbeard first sailed south to the Bay of Honduras where he formed an uneasy alliance with Stede Bonnet, a wealthy planter from Barbados who had turned pirate. Now Blackbeard commanded a formidable fleet. Besides his ship and Bonnet's he had a heavy trading vessel, another sloop, and two smaller ships. Aboard these vessels were 400 well armed pirates. Blackbeard now headed for Charleston in South Carolina. Charleston at the time was one of the richest cities in the colonies. A constant stream of ships flowed between her harbor and the various ports of Europe. Blackbeard blockaded Charleston harbor and in a short time captured nine ships. Aboard the last ship he took was a Mr. Samuel Wragg, a member of the Council of the Governor of South Carolina. Blackbeard ransomed him for a chest of medicines. It was a curious ransom demand, especially as a large sum probably would have been paid for Mr. Wragg, and the medicine chest was valued at only £300. Two theories have since been put forward to explain this unusual ransom: the first that Blackbeard was a drug addict and needed laudanum because he was going through withdrawal; the second that his most recent "wife" had left him with a venereal disease to remember her by. The governor of South Carolina paid the ransom, and Blackbeard kept his part of the bargain by not chopping off Mr. Wragg's head. At this point Blackbeard double-crossed Bonnet. He had the best of the plunder transferred onto a smaller, faster sloop, on which he sailed away.

Stede Bonnet sailed on to Bath and accepted a pardon. Then, having a sudden and dramatic change of heart, went in pursuit of Blackbeard with a ship full of angry men searching for Blackbeard, determined to have revenge. In the meantime, Blackbeard came and went freely along the coast of Florida, Georgia, and the Carolinas. Finally, the residents had had enough. No ship in the area was safe. Since Governor Eden was involved in shady business deals with Blackbeard, they turned for help to his neighbor, Governor Alexander Spotswood of Virginia. Governor Spotswood summoned captains Brand and Gordon, who each commanded a British warship stationed in the James River. Their men-of-war were too large to maneuver in the Ocracoke inlet and give chase among the shoals of Pamlico Sound. They agreed, however, to provide the leadership and crews if Governor Spotswood would provide the proper type of ships, in this case sloops. Spotswood agreed to finance the purchase of the sloops and even went a step further. He had legislation passed that put a price on the pirates' heads. Blackbeard was the only pirate cited by name, and the price on his head was far larger than that offered for the other pirates.

Blackbeard now set up base in the town of Bath. Across the sound he installed his fourteenth, and final bride, in a grand mansion. He stayed there for long periods, occasionally returning to his sloop in Ocracoke's harbor. While Blackbeard enjoyed a life of ease, the two warships sent by Governor Spotswood and commanded by a Lieutenant Maynard were heading toward his Ocracoke hideout determined to bring him to justice dead or alive.

Meanwhile Blackbeard laughed off reports of the approaching enemy. He had begun to think of himself as invincible. When Maynard arrived, he stationed his two sloops off the harbor. Escape seemed impossible. Blackbeard was trapped.

In characteristic fashion, Blackbeard's preparations for battle included getting roaring drunk. The crews on both sides of the battle line passed a tense night. With the first light of morning, Blackbeard, the most infamous pirate in the Americas, rounded the bend and came into view. Now all young Lieutenant Maynard had to do was to go in and capture him.

Blackbeard, however, was ready for him. His sloop was small, fast and heavily gunned. Maynard could see Blackbeard towering over the rest of his crew, with his favorite cutlass, a heavy razor-sharp meat cleaver, hung at his side. As the two sloops attempted to close in on Blackbeard, he began to maneuver his craft, displaying his intimate knowledge of the Ocracoke's harbor and its many shoals and sandbars. Because both of Maynard's ships were in close pursuit, Blackbeard was able to practically guide them onto a sandbar and run them both aground. Now with His Majesty's ships laid up, Blackbeard was free to run for the open sea. But rather than leave Maynard's sloops free to resume their chase as soon as the high tide returned and lifted them off the sandbar, Blackbeard decided to teach the Royal Navy a lesson. Blackbeard ordered the heavy guns on his ships to be loaded with grapeshot, spikes, iron bars, and chain. The enemy's sails were shredded and her masts splintered. Nine men were killed outright or died agonizingly painful deaths.

Although he deeply enjoyed watching this destruction, Blackbeard's howls of laughter soon turned to profane screams launched at the

OPPOSITE — Blackbeard's last fight. Howard Pyle.

127

Blackbeard's head hung from the yardarm. Nineteenth century engraving.

heavens. His own ship had become stuck on the same sandbar as Maynard's. The few minutes it had taken him to fire his guns was just enough time for the breeze and tide to conspire to run his ship aground. Blackbeard had been trapped in his own web, Maynard lightened his ship sufficiently to free it from the sandbar and came directly for Blackbeard's sloop. A well aimed broadside did great damage, but he turned to come round again for another direct attack. Maynard's boat drew closer; Blackbeard, seeing only two or three sailors on deck, gave the order to board her and cut them to pieces. Once aboard, the pirates realized they had been deceived. After the broadside Maynard had ordered the majority of his crew to go below deck. It was a perfect trap. There were now actually 30 well armed sailors facing 23 pirates.

What followed may well have been the bloodiest battle in the history of piracy. Men cut and slashed one another in hand-to-hand combat. Blackbeard, mangled and bloody from the fighting, took a bullet in his shoulder that slowed but did not stop him. Suddenly, as Blackbeard was about to slice Lieutenant Maynard in two, a sailor heaved a pike at Blackbeard from behind. It caught him between the right shoulder and the ear. A second blow caught him squarely on the forehead. The huge man was dazed and could barely see through the blood that flowed freely down his face and through his long beard. By now, all the pirates had surrendered and quit the fight. Nearly the entire crew of Maynard's ship was gathered in a joint attack on Blackbeard. Repeated jabs, cuts, and slashes could not seem to stop the crazed pirate captain. It was a macabre scene. This enormous ghastly looking man oozing blood, his flesh ripped to shreds, just kept swinging his cutlass with all the fury of the Devil defending Hell. Finally, it was over, Blackbeard collapsed dead. Lieutenant Maynard ordered his head chopped off and hung from the bowsprit as a warning to anyone who would dare question the authority of His Majesty's Royal Navy.

The survivors of Blackbeard's crew were all convicted of piracy and hanged.

Anne Bonny
Mary Read and
Calico Jack

Most of us are not surprised to discover that throughout history there have been exceptional women who, in spite of prevailing social conditions, have excelled in endeavors political, economic, and religious. The story of Anne Bonny and Mary Read lends a new twist to that phrase. Why should there not have been members of the fairer sex who, seeking fortune, took to the seas with the same enthusiasm for plunder and pillage as their male counterparts? Indeed there were two such women. Interestingly enough, their stories are closely intertwined.

Anne Bonny found her way to New Providence as the newlywed of a young seaman, who deserted his young bride shortly after their arrival on the island. However, far from being upset at her abandonment, Anne took to New Providence with great enthusiasm. Before long she met a dashing young pirate captain, John Rackham, whose fondness for calico pants had earned him the name "Calico Jack." Rackham was so enamored of Bonny that he refused to leave her. This presented a problem since tradition barred women from pirate ships. Most pirate ships' articles clearly stated that bringing a woman on board was punishable by death. Calico Jack asked Anne to disguise herself as a man and come with him, and she readily agreed.

OPPOSITE — John Rackham (Calico Jack). Engraving from the Library of Congress.

Rackham's career had begun as the sun of piracy was already slipping past its zenith. His story is a rather sad one. Instead of hauling in rich prizes of gold doubloons and jewels, he was at times reduced to stealing fishermen's nets or livestock from the mainland. In all he fared far better at collecting women than he did treasure. On a two-year cruise through the West Indies, he ended up with only "50 rolls of tobacco and Nine bags of Piemento." Not very much to show for two years "on the account."

Early in his career Rackham served as quartermaster in Captain Charlie Vane's company. After Vane had run from a fight with a well-armed French ship, he was dismissed from command and marooned on an uninhabited island off the coast of Central America. The crew elected Rackham to be their captain in his place. This was on November 24, 1718, and on the very first day of his command he had the good fortune to take and plunder several small vessels, endearing himself to his crew and getting his career as a captain off to a good start.

Christmas was approaching, and the pirates were in an appropriately festive mood. They landed on a small island to celebrate the holiday, carousing and drinking as long as the liquor lasted.

Their next encounter was a strange one. They came alongside a ship that surrendered without putting up any resistance upon seeing Rackham's black flag. The pirates who boarded her in order to inspect the crew and cargo found that she was transporting thieves from Newgate Prison to a life of indentured servitude on the plantations of the Caribbean and the southern colonies of North America. Pirates had a general aversion to slavery and the practice of indentured servitude and were happy for an opportunity to free such unfortunates. After disposing of the guards, Rackham offered the prisoners the chance to sign his articles, thereby gaining many new recruits. Adding the two vessels to his own to form a small flotilla, Rackham sailed to the Bahamas. It was at this point that he crossed paths with Anne Bonny.

With Anne aboard, Rackham's ship went on a four-month cruise. During this time they managed to conceal her true sex. But Rackham's luck began to change for the worse. Woodes Rogers had become governor at New Providence, and his determined opposition had made the seas much more inhospitable to the business of piracy. The governor sent a sloop after him that successfully deprived him of his recently acquired prizes.

Soon after Anne discovered that she was pregnant. Rackham now sailed his ship to a snug little cove he knew of in Cuba. He left Anne there to deliver her baby, which apparently she never wanted to see again once she had given birth to it. Returning for Anne, he found himself in awkward situation and was only able to collect her at great peril to himself and his crew. Just as they were about to set sail, a Spanish man-of-war accompanied by a recently taken English sloop sailed into the cove. Rackham was now unable to get past the Spanish ship; all he could do was to hide behind an islet in the cove. When the sun set, with the dark blanket of the Caribbean night covering his movements, Rackham loaded all his crew into a boat, rowed stealthily up to the sloop, clambered aboard and threatened instant death to the Spanish guards if they cried out. Then he cut the cables and sailed out of the bay. As soon as the sun rose, the Spanish realized that their prize was gone. They commenced a furious bombardment of Rackham's empty vessel, thinking he was still aboard her.

Now, Anne shipped openly as a woman. It is said that Rackham gave his crew the ultimatum that either they accept the fact or sail without him.

Shortly after this, Rackham heard about the king's amnesty and he, along with Anne, went ashore at New Providence and took the pardon. Rackham remained at New Providence until his money was spent and then signed onto an honest privateer fitted to go out against the hated Spanish. Anne, once again disguised as a man, went with him. Only a few days out of port, Rackham and Bonny incited the privateer's crew to mutiny and took command of the vessel. Aboard the privateer-turned-pirate was a handsome young man who attracted Anne's attention, the first to divert her from Rackham. Gradually, so as not to excite Rackham's jealousy, she started up a friendship with him. She noticed his bravery in battle and became more and more infatuated. As soon as she had an occasion to be alone with him, Anne took the opportunity to let him know that she was a woman. Much to her surprise the object of her affections turned out to be the same.

Mary Read was born in London to a poor family. She began her career as a male impersonator at a young age when she signed on a man-of-war as a cabin boy. Mary was also said to have served in the regular army and to have run a successful tavern. When the tavern failed she tried to reenlist; but the peacetime army was far too tame for her. Once again she donned her disguise and shipped aboard a Dutch vessel headed for the West Indies.

As luck would have it, her ship was taken by pirates before she reached her destination. The ship's articles showed that she was the only Englishman aboard. As the pirates were all English themselves, they insisted she join their company. She proved herself to be extremely adept at hiding the secret of her sex, but she only had to maintain her disguise

OVERLEAF — Anne Bonny and Mary Read. From Johnson's *A General History of Pirates*.

for a short time before the pirates got news of the king's offer of amnesty. They put into New Providence forthwith to enjoy their ill-gotten gains. That is how Mary came to be at New Providence.

After her adventurous life, Mary too, found life on land intolerably dull. So it was that when the privateer sailed out against the Spanish, Anne Bonny, Calico Jack, and Mary Read were all on board.

Anne Bonny's attentions to Mary Read had not gone unnoticed by Calico Jack. He had decided to cut the "fellow's" throat, but Anne learned of his plan and revealed Mary's true identity to Rackham. He decided to go along with the charade, rightly fearing trouble if the rest of the crew found out that there were two women aboard.

In time Mary herself fell in love with one of the crew and began a long affair with him. One night Mary's lover got into a fight with one of his shipmates. The quarrel ended with a challenge to a duel. Mary, fearing for the safety of her lover, quickly started an argument with her lover's opponent and challenged him to a duel as well. On shore, the combat began with single-shot pistols; both parties missed. Then they fell to with their cutlasses. After a long and bloody fight, Mary cut down the other and left him to die in the sand.

In October 1720 Rackham was preying on the island of Jamaica. He had taken several ships and was leading raids against coastal towns. The entire island was up in arms and had pleaded with the governor, Sir Nicholas Lawes, to take some action. In response Lawes fitted out a sloop-of-war, commanded by Captain Barnet to pursue and capture the marauding pirate. Barnet came upon Rackham near Negril Bay and found a captain and crew drunk from imbibing rum captured aboard a fisherman's vessel. The pirates were capable of only a half-hearted defense, and they were boarded by Barnet's crew. One by one they surrendered and were driven below. When the battle ended, only two pirates remained on deck, swinging and slashing and swearing at their shipmates to come up and fight like men. The two were Anne Bonny and Mary Read. It took nearly Barnet's entire crew to subdue the two and confine them.

Rackham and his crew were brought to Port Royal, tried, found guilty, and sentenced to death. The judge asked each pirate if there was any reason why the death sentence should not be enforced. Suddenly one of them, motioning to herself and a companion said. "My Lord, we plead our bellies." A doctor was sent for to examine the two pirates. After a quick examination the doctor returned to the court and said that the two were indeed women and that both were pregnant. As a result the judge commuted their death sentences.

Mary Read's lover was hanged. Mary herself died shortly after in prison of a violent fever. She never repented. Asked if she didn't regret a life that could only lead to the gallows, she replied that were it not for the fear of hanging, every sailor on the high seas would turn pirate and ruin the trade for the good ones.

No one knows what became of Anne Bonny, but it is believed that she was freed and sent home to her father who had become a wealthy planter in the Carolinas. Her last meeting with her lover, Calico Jack, was a bitter one. On his way to the gallows his guards did him the favor of allowing him to see Anne one last time. When he stood chained in the doorway of her cell she greeted him by saying, "I'm sorry to see you in this situation, but if you had fought like a man you need not have died like a dog." Rackham was hanged on November 17 1720, at Gallows Point, Port Royal.

Major Stede Bonnet sporting the powdered wig of a gentleman. Contemporary engraving (Library of Congress).

Gentleman
Stede Bonnet

Fictional accounts of piracy abound with aristocratic figures who take to life on the high seas for adventure or to revenge some injustice worked upon them. Such were the romantic heroes of Byron's *The Corsair* and Errol Flynn's *Captain Blood*. But almost none of the noteworthy Caribbean pirates, came from the upper classes. Born the scion of one of England's great wealthy families, Stede Bonnet was an unlikely candidate for the role of pirate captain. He was the owner of a vast and prosperous plantation on the island of Barbados and a pillar of the island's community and church. In marked contrast to most pirates, whose impoverished backgrounds were natural breeding grounds for outlaws and adventurers, Bonnet was a true aristocrat who served as an officer in the king's army and retired with the gentleman's rank of major. Bonnet departed from the rule of pirates in another significant way: he reportedly was subject to bouts of seasickness.

In the entire history of Caribbean piracy Bonnet was the only pirate known to have purchased his own ship. He bought a sloop, outfitted it with ten heavy guns, recruited 70 crewmen and christened the vessel, *Revenge*, a favorite name for pirate ships.

It has been suggested that Bonnet's wife drove him to a life of crime. She was an absolute harridan and, compared to her incessant nagging, plying the trade of a pirate seemed most inviting.

Bonnet set sail for the coast of North America and the rich trade routes between the colonies and England. His crew, unaccustomed to someone whose background did not encourage drunkenness, profanity and debauchery, at first were insubordinate. This was compounded by his seasickness and limited knowledge of nautical science. His army training, however, proved useful for dealing with a ship full of cutthroats and ruffians, and he soon became known as a firm disciplinarian.

Bonnet and the *Revenge* arrived off the coast of Virginia and began their hunt with incredibly good luck. They took two prizes, two lumbering, virtually unarmed merchantman, in as many days. Following the capture of two additional ships, the *Revenge* was overflowing both with goods and captives. Then Bonnet set sail not for Barbados, or New Providence, the pirate headquarters of the Caribbean, but for Long Island Sound, New York.

Just within the protection of the jaws of Long Island lies Gardiners Island, which has served as a way station for pirates for three centuries. This small island was deeded to the Gardiners by a land grant from Charles II and is held by the same family to this day. It has hidden coves that make it an ideal stopover point for pirate ships. In addition, it is within rowing distance of Long Island and the highway that ran straight to New York. Because dealing in pirate plunder was so profitable there were many unscrupulous New York merchants who were happy to act as go-betweens. However, the punishment was harsh for those caught engaging in this trade. This made the somewhat remote location of Gardiners Island ideal for unloading contraband. It could then be rowed across to Long Island and taken overland into New York City. From a huge hill on the middle of the island lookouts could easily spot any approaching ships which looked like pirate chasers. From Gardiners Island to the open Atlantic was a quick run making escape easy.

After haggling with the middlemen and selling his cargo of rum, sugar, scotch, tweed, and other commodities, Bonnet left Gardiners Island to resume his hunt for prizes. Coming upon what looked like a promising catch, Bonnet was unpleasantly surprised when the other ship unfurled its blood-red flag of skull and cross bones. The ship belonged to Blackbeard. Although Bonnet at Blackbeard's invitation joined forces with him, the reality of the situation was that Bonnet was more of a prisoner than a partner. Blackbeard took him aboard his ship and placed one of his own lieutenants in command of Bonnet's ship. Bonnet's run with Blackbeard was profitable and lasted until Blackbeard decided to shed the excess weight of a fleet and returned Bonnet to command of his own ship and let him leave. In the process he made off with the lion's share of the loot they had both amassed.

Serving with Blackbeard not only turned Bonnet's stomach but changed his mind about a life of piracy. Now that he was once again in command of his own ship he headed straight for North Carolina where he sought and received the royal pardon from the governor, Charles Eden.

Soon after, news reached the Carolinas that war had once again broken out between Spain and England. Bonnet decided to sail for the West Indies in the hopes of obtaining a privateer's license, legally entitling him to attack ships belonging to Spain. But overcome by his obsessive desire for revenge against Blackbeard, he changed course and chased him to

Stede Bonnet upon the gallows. From Johnson's *A General History of Pirates*.

Ocracoke. His opponent, however, proved too wily for him. Once again Bonnet made an about face and decided to return to piracy. He looted several ships off Virginia and in Delaware Bay. Since he had recently taken the pardon, he changed his name to Captain Thomas, and that of his sloop to the *Royal James*.

In order to carry out needed repairs on his ship, Bonnet sailed up the Cape Fear River in North Carolina and spent nearly two months there. News of his whereabouts reached Charleston, South Carolina. There another ex-army officer named William Rhett, asked for and received a commission to arrest Bonnet. With two sloops outfitted as men-of-war Rhett trapped Bonnet in the Cape Fear River. After a ferocious battle, Rhett prevailed and captured Bonnet and his entire crew. Brought to Charleston as a prisoner, Bonnet, unlike the rest of his crew, was treated with the privileges due to a person of his station. His guard was inordinately light, as his captors expected him to behave like a gentleman. Bonnet, however, could clearly see that his future led to the gallows. Somehow, either by bribery or chicanery, he managed to evade his guards and together with his sailing master, David Herriot, escape to the waterfront. There the two stole a small boat and escaped to sea. The escape created a scandal for Governor Johnson of South Carolina, who was already suspected of illegal dealings with pirates. To quell the growing indignation, he offered a reward of £700 for the capture of Bonnet dead or alive. Again the biggest search party was lead by William Rhett.

Bonnet was captured within the week and this time placed under heavy guard in Charleston. Meanwhile the crew of the *Royal James* had gone on trial. All were found guilty, and all but three sentenced to death. On Saturday, November 8, 1718, 22 of Bonnet's crew followed the admiralty court's traditional silver oar to the gallows and were hanged. It was and still remains one of the biggest mass executions in the city's history.

Bonnet's trial followed two days later. He was found guilty of taking eleven vessels and killing 18 innocent seamen, all since accepting the king's pardon. The judge, although loath to sentence a fellow aristocrat to death, did precisely that. Bonnet was hanged by the neck till dead.

No one knows for certain why a wealthy plantation owner would give up comfort and respectability for an uncomfortable and risky life that more often than not ended ignominiously. His career does, however, suggest that there was a real attraction in the excitement and freedom from restraint that a life on the high seas offered in what was a rather formal and rigid age. At any rate it is one thing for an impoverished seaman to take up piracy; for an aristocrat to risk everything is quite another story.

Captain

Joseph Thwaites

Joseph Thwaites was one of the most savage of the pirates who ever terrorized the Barbary Coast. He began his career in the Royal Navy as coxswain to Captain Hood, on the HMS *Zealous*. Thwaites was promoted in 1763 to midshipman. The ship was ordered to patrol the Mediterranean Sea. Putting into Algiers, Thwaites went ashore to buy some sheep and never returned. The captain assumed he had been assassinated and sailed without him. The fact was that Thwaites, who spoke both Turkish and Greek, accepted an offer to enter the service of the Ottoman Bey. He embraced Islam without any reservations and was put in charge of a 44-gun frigate. His first engagement was with the flagship of the Tunisian fleet, which he took and carried to Algiers.

Once Thwaites soiled his hand with blood, he seemed to take to it with great enthusiasm. He attacked and took vessels of any nation, drowning all his prisoners by tying a double-headed shot round their necks and throwing them overboard.

He stopped at no atrocity — even children were killed. He murdered an old shipmate of his, an English lieutenant named Roberts, without a second thought.

For several years this highly successful pirate plundered ships of all nations until such pressure was brought upon the Bey of Algiers that Thwaites thought it best to collect what valuables he could carry away and disappear.

Landing in Gibraltar in 1796, dressed in European clothes, he procured passage to New York in an American frigate, the *Constitution*. Arriving in the United States, he purchased an estate not far from New York and built himself a handsome mansion, but a year later retribution came from an unlooked-for quarter. He was bitten by a rattlesnake and died in the most horrible agonies of mind and body.

Life on the High Seas

Pirate Ships

Nothing was more indispensable to the pirates than the ships they sailed. The ship was not only the chief instrument of their piracy, without which they could not have carried out their attacks, it was also their home, transportation, and means of escape.

Most pirates stole their ships during attacks or came across them as a result of mutiny. The case of Calico Jack and Anne Bonny, described above, is just one of many instances in which a dissatisfied crew took possession of a ship. There were also many cases in which ships were purchased and outfitted for privateering and ended up as pirate vessels. Most pirates preferred to stay with one ship. However, some captains switched ships several times, some out of necessity, others out of personal preference. Bartholomew Roberts, for example, changed ships six times in three years.

From ancient times, pirates have favored small, light ships. These allowed them to escape larger galleons. The early buccaneers raided in sloops or small frigates frequently captured from Spanish traders. When Sir Henry Morgan sailed for Panama in 1670, his men were packed into 38 small vessels. The largest, Morgan's 120-ton flagship carried only 140 men. During the early eighteenth century, Atlantic pirates cruised in sloops and in schooners, even on long distance voyages to Africa and Madagascar. A few captured and sailed in brigantines and three-masted square-riggers.

It is important at this point to bear in mind the vast improvements in the construction of sailing vessels during the period in question. As the maritime historian, Hans Bathe, notes in *Seven Centuries of Sea Travel*:

OPPOSITE — *Royal Sovereign*. An outstanding example of seventeenth-century shipbuilding, painted by Willem van de Velde the Younger. The van de Veldes, father and son, were the preeminent maritime painters of their day. (National Maritime Museum, London).

The simple arrangement of six sails — courses and topsails on fore and main masts, lateen sails on the mizzen mast and spritsail under the bowsprit — at first fitted to the three masts, was gradually improved with the introduction of topgallant sails, royal sails, jibs, stay sails, studding sails and the substitution of a gaff sail for the lateen sail, until, by the end of the eighteenth century, 37 sails formed the sail plan of even a small merchant ship.

Pirates, whose business was to prey upon merchant shipping, had to keep up with these developments. Since surprise and a speedy escape were key to their success, they needed small fast ships to catch merchantmen and escape pursuers. Ships of smaller size had an additional advantage. They were able to enter shallow waters or sail across reefs where warships were unable to follow. Blackbeard in his final battle relied upon the shallow draw of his sloop and his superior knowledge of the coast to elude pursuit. A navigational mistake cost him his life.

Finally, and just as important, smaller ships were easier to maintain. One of the primary elements of proper maintenance was careening. Careening involves turning a ship onto its side, so that its bottom can be cleaned or repaired; this adds greatly to the speed of sailing vessels. Clearly smaller ships were easier to careen. Pirates sought safe havens to careen their vessels. This was usually an exceptionally anxious time because the ship's guns had to be taken ashore. Secured with block and tackle to sturdy trees on the shore, the ship was completely vulnerable to the sudden approach of a government warship.

Today the word "sloop" has a definite meaning: a sailing vessel with a fore-and-aft rig. (A square rigged sail is perpendicular to the length of the ship as opposed to fore-and-aft rigging which is parallel.) During the seventeenth and eighteenth centuries the term was used more loosely and described a wide variety of small ships. An American designed variation on the sloop, called the schooner, was developed in the United States at the very beginning of the eighteenth century.

The profitable trade of attacking merchantmen in the West Indies gave rise to the demand for vessels fast enough to escape capture. The shipbuilders of Jamaica rose to the challenge and developed a sloop which acquired a well-deserved reputation for seaworthiness and speed. The Jamaica sloop was built of red cedar and became easily identifiable for that reason.

Similar in appearance and equally renowned for her speed was the Bermuda sloop, which was built in considerable numbers. Privateers also made use of the Bermuda built schooner.

While marine painting was coming into its own during this period, as seen in the works of the Dutch masters van de Velde, father and son, there are for all intents and purposes no contemporary pictures of particular

ABOVE — Pirates ashore for careening. Careening had to be done frequently in the tropics due to the abundance of marine growths. From Johnson's *A General History of Pirates*.

OVERLEAF — *Embarkation of Henry VIII*. Three-masted lateen rigged carracks of the early sixteenth century. Large seaworthy vessels of this kind made possible the exploration of the New World. S. H. Grimm (National Maritime Museum, London).

English frigate with all sails rigged. Eighteenth century. Bonjean. (Musée de la Marine, Giraudon/Art Resource, N.Y.).

French barques, *L'Astrolabe* and *Le Zèle*. Le Breton. (Musée de la Marine, Giaraudon, Art Resource, N.Y.)

A single-masted sloop of the late eighteenth century. Pirates favored these small craft for their maneuverability, speed and low maintenance (Peabody Essex Museum, Salem, Mass.).

pirate ships reliably drawn. The engraving of Bartholomew Roberts with the *Royal Fortune* and captured slave ships in the background [see page 54] is one of the better ones, but here the artist seems more interested in the ship's flags than its rigging. Known pirate vessels did not frequent the harbors in which the marine painters normally worked. Nor did they as a rule seek out publicity. But as they pretty much sailed in what they could find, pictures of contemporary merchant vessels provide a fair idea of what their ships must have looked like.

Although armaments were extremely important aboard a pirate ship, pirates would not be deterred from taking a poorly armed vessel because they could, and usually did, refit the ships to suit their needs and liking.

One of the first things done by pirates upon taking a ship was to undertake alterations in order to prepare the ship for their own use. According to Captain Johnson's *General History of the Pirates*, after taking a ship they began, "making such alterations as might fit her for a Sea Rover, pulling down her bulkheads, and making her flush, so that she

Le Royal Louis. A French 64-gun galley. Its three masts are fully rigged and the bowsprit carries a jib sail. M. Rodoelme, 1667 (Giraudon/Art Resource, N.Y.).

La Wagram. French warship of 100 guns. Joseph-Ange Antoine Roux. (Peabody Essex Museum, Salem, Mass.).

became, in all respects, as complete a ship for their purpose as any they could have found." That is, they would take a ship, much of whose interior space had been divided up into compartments for carrying cargo, and eliminate any obstructions that got in the way of its fighting ability. Often times a pirate captain would order his ship disguised. Its gun ports would be covered over in hope that she would be taken for an innocuous merchantman. At the same time many merchantmen would paint on an additional row of gun ports and pretend they were well-armed men-of-war.

Though most pirates favored smaller ships, there were advantages to a larger ship — large ships were more seaworthy and provided a platform for more guns. Many pirates, including Bartholomew Roberts and Charlie Vane sailed in ships. In these they could take on most merchant vessels, which were as a rule undermanned — the priority of merchant ship owners was always to maximize profits by reducing their overhead. Pirates on the other hand had no overhead since there was no pay as such. They signed on knowing that they would be paid only when plunder was taken. Consequently pirate crews typically outnumbered those of their prey and that gave them a terrific advantage in hand-to-hand combat.

Experiment of Newbury Port. A two-masted brigantine, square rigged. Many pirates sailed in ships such as these. Nicolas Cammillieri (Peabody Essex Musuem, Salem, Mass.).

Louisa. Privateer's tops'l schooner of Bermuda. Schooners were built for speed. Note the fore-and-aft rigging in contrast to the brigantine. Giuseppe Fedi (Peabody Essex Musuem, Salem, Mass.).

FAMOUS PIRATE SHIPS AND THEIR CAPTAINS

Black Joke	Captain Benito de Soto
Bravo	Captain Power
Flying Horse	Captain Rhoade
Fortune	Captain Bartholomew Roberts
Royal Fortune	Captain Bartholomew Roberts
Good Fortune	Captain Bartholomew Roberts
Bachelor's Delight	Captain William Dampier
Delight	Captain Francis Spriggs
Flying King	Captain Sample
Night Rambler	Captain Cooper
Cour Valant	Captain La Vivion
Most Holy Trinity	Captain Bartholomew Sharp
Flying Dragon	Captain Edmund Condent
Sudden Death	Captain Derdrake
Scowerer	Captain Evans
Queen Anne's Revenge	Captain Edward Teach (Blackbeard)
Happy Delivery	Captain George Lowther
Snap Dragon	Captain Goldsmith
Revenge	Captains Cowley, Bonnet, Gow, Phillips, and others
Blessing	Captain Brown
New York Revenge	Captain Cole
Mayflower	Captain Cox
Childhood	Captain Caraccioli
Liberty	Captain Thomas Tew

OVERLEAF — A three-masted sloop flying the black flag of piracy engages a merchant ship. Thomas Buttersworth (Peabody Essex Museum, Salem, Mass.).

Pirate Codes

While people tend to think of the pirates as wild, lawless villains, they were in some respects quite well organized. In fact Caribbean piracy actually provides examples of one of the Americas' first experiments in democracy. In general a pirate ship was owned by its crew, and the division of all prizes was spelled out and agreed to beforehand. The captain was usually elected to his office and could also be voted out if the crew became dissatisfied with his performance. Although the captain had complete and absolute authority when the ship was engaged in battle and could enforce the death penalty on a crew member who did not follow orders, as soon as the fighting ceased the same captain could be deposed by a simple majority vote. The other elected officer was the quartermaster. He shared power with the captain and was second in command. His duties included supervising the operation of the ship, except when in battle, and deciding what plunder to take and what to let go. He was in charge of all the loot taken until it was divided and then presided over its distribution and settled the arguments which inevitably arose. The quartermaster, like the captain, served at the will of the crew and could be voted out of office at any time. Many of the pirates had suffered under the heavy hand of tyrannical captains in the merchant service and the navy, and they protected their rights on board by effectively splitting the command.

Ordinarily the other officers serving on a pirate ship were appointed by the captain or the quartermaster. The boatswain was in charge of the ship's maintenance, sails, tackle, supplies, etc. The gunner supervised his

ARTICLES OF BARTHOLOMEW ROBERTS

1. Every man has a vote in affairs of moment; has equal title to the fresh provisions, or strong liquors, at any time seized, and may use them at pleasure, unless a scarcity, makes it necessary, for the good of all, to vote a retrenchment.

2. Every man to be called fairly in turn, by list, on board of prizes, because, (over and above their proper share) they were on these occasions allowed a shift of clothes: but if they defrauded the company to the value of a dollar in plate, jewels or money, marooning was the punishment. If the robbery was only betwixt one another, they contented themselves with slitting the ears and nose of him that was guilty, and set him on shore, not in an uninhabited place, but somewhere, where he was sure to encounter hardships.

3. No person to game at cards or dice for money.

4. The lights and candles to be put out at eight o'clock at night: if any of the crew, after that hour still remained inclined for drinking, they were to do it on the open deck.

5. To keep their piece, pistols, and cutlass clean and fit for service.

6. No boy or woman to be allowed amongst them. If any man were to be found seducing any of the latter sex, and carried her to sea, disguised, he was to suffer death.

7. To desert the ship or their quarters in battle, was punished with death or marooning.

8. No striking one another on board, but every man's quarrels to be ended on shore, at sword and pistol.

9. No man to talk of breaking up their way of living until each had shared £1,000. If in order to this, any man should lose a limb, or become a cripple in their service, he was to have 800 dollars, out of the public stock, and for lesser hurts proportionately.

10. The captain and the quartermaster to receive two shares of a prize: the master, boatswain, and gunner, one share and a half, and other officers one and a quarter.

11. The musicians to have rest on the Sabbath Day, but the other six days and nights, none without special favor.

OVERLEAF — Vivid portrayal of the marooned pirate. Howard Pyle.

own crew at the ship's armament. The sailing master was in charge of navigation. Some of the bigger pirate vessels even carried a surgeon, a sailmaker, and a carpenter, all of whom had a vital role to play in maintaining the well being of the ship and the crew.

Every pirate ship followed a set of rules or "articles" that were actually written and agreed upon by all parties before the ship ever set sail. Quite a few different examples of ship's articles have been preserved. Those drawn up by the men led by Bartholomew Roberts are stricter than some, but they provide a revealing look at the pirate's life at sea. They are quoted above from Captain Johnson's *General History of the Pirates*.

Whatever the variations, these codes were strictly adhered to. The pirates had turned their backs on the law of nations and the near absolute powers granted to captains at sea. Instead, they set about establishing their own constitutions in a democratic fashion almost a century before the American and French revolutions.

Pirate Flags

While the precise origin of the pirate flag remains unknown, there is some history to its evolution. What is certain is that nothing could conjure fear and dread more readily than the swift approach of a pirate flag. Knowing this, pirates seemed to make full use of the flag as a weapon to psychologically affect their prey. For instance, Bartholomew Roberts displayed a double threat with two flags. One depicted the captain and a skeleton drinking a toast to death. On the other Roberts let his hatred for the islands of Barbados and Martinique be known by picturing himself astride two skulls labeled "ABH" and "AMH" — "A Barbadian's Head" and "A Martinican's Head."

Identifying an enemy at sea has always been difficult. In ancient times sailors might have been able to recognize an enemy by the color of the vessel's sail, or by a device painted on the sail. Designs on the shields of the soldiers aboard a ship might have been used for purposes of identification. In the mosaics in the ancient Roman port of Ostia, banners and standards can be seen on ships. Such flags have commonly been used for identification of ships.

Streamers, pennants, and flags of identity appear on both merchant and warships early in the Middle Ages. In the 1200s long, flowing pennants or streamers, began to appear on ships. At sea they could indicate nationality or personal identity as well as a state of hostility. By the late 1300s these streamers were sometimes longer than 30 yards, and were very wide with complicated designs embroidered or painted on them. In 1416, for instance, the Earl of Warwick's identifying streamer showed a bear with a ragged staff, together with crosses and slashes having various meanings connected with his coat of arms. Henry VIII of England had the sails of one of his vessels painted gold, and had the streamers on it painted green and white, the Tudor colors, with the cross of St. George.

Original
Jolly Roger

Captain Condent

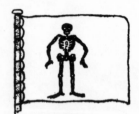

Modified
Jolly Roger

Captain
Emanuel Wynne

French Jolly Roger

Captain
Edward England

Captain
Christopher Moody

Captain Bartholomew Roberts

In the late 1600s it was common for privateers to fly their national flag, as well as a special streamer that identified them as privateers. In the 1690s a law was passed in England making the flying of such streamers mandatory. Privateering streamers were hoisted for the very practical reason that, knowing the privateer's intent, the captain of a merchant ship could strike his own colors quickly, and thus avoid having his ship battered by cannon. Before the 1700s pirates hoisted a red flag prior to attack, to show their intent. This came to be known as sailing "under the Red Jack." Sometime in the late 1600s the black pirate pennant began to appear. The black flag was raised after the Red Jack if the vessel the pirates intended to capture indicated resistance.

These red and black flags — sometimes they were yellow — were described simply as the Black Flag, or the Roger, or Old Roger. Roger was the slang expression for vagabond, derived from the legal term "rouge" used in the rouge laws against wandering beggars in England. Late in the 1600s and early in the 1700s, the more flamboyant privateers and pirates began to add various symbols to their flags. Often the symbol of choice was the skull, sometimes depicted with crossed bones, the ancient symbol of danger and death. But, skeletons, spears, hourglasses, initials, crossed cutlasses, and many other symbols were also used. One such flag depicted a skeleton with either crossed swords or bones in one hand, and in the other a glass of grog, which indicated the crew was ready for business and primed for the attack. Shortly after the appearance of this device the flag used by pirates was commonly referred to as the Jolly Roger. The use of such flags was limited, however, for the common practice of pirates of the period was to show false colors, and attack in surprise. Pirates sometimes went to great lengths to disguise their identity and gain the element of surprise. Sometimes they went as far as donning women's clothing, and prancing around deck with parasols.

OPPOSITE — Flags of a number of notorious pirates

OVERLEAF — Pirates on deck masquerading as women in preparation for an attack on a ship. Note the musician at the center perched on a barrel. Musicians were standard fixtures in pirate crews. Artist unknown. (Peabody Essex Museum, Salem, Mass.).

Wrecks and Wrecking

Laws concerning wrecks can be traced back to ancient Rhodes. They stipulated that a wreck belonged to the noble on whose coast the ship foundered. Owners, however, had three months to claim the wreck if there were survivors aboard. Then, by custom, a portion of the ship's cargo was given to the local lord for the time and trouble involved in the transaction.

During the late Middle Ages ships still mainly traveled from "view to view." Staying close to the coast often led to grounding on reefs and rocks not known to the navigator. New wrecking laws introduced among the emerging Italian port cities during the thirteenth and fourteenth centuries as part of an expanded maritime code were also adopted in the north. Underlying these wrecking laws was the principle that if any person or animal were alive when the wreck was found, the ship was not to be considered abandoned; therefore, it was not open to claim by anyone but the proper shareholders. Previously in the north a local lord claimed any wreck discovered on his territory. Any merchandise on a wrecked vessel became his, and surviving passengers and crewmen became his prisoners, sometimes for many years. These prisoners were held as hostages in exchange for prisoners held by the ruler of the country from which the passengers and crew came. Sometimes they were sold as slaves and sometimes they were ransomed. The new laws concerning wrecks changed these practices. In regions where wrecking was a tradition, however, the change was hardly for the better, for the new laws lead to the death of innocent voyagers who survived a shipwreck only to be killed by wreckers so that the vessel could be claimed as an abandoned one.

Purposely wrecking ships was an extremely lucrative form of piracy. Luring a ship into shallow or rocky waters by the use of false beacons was common practice along certain coasts. Penalties for wrecking varied from country to country. If it were proven that human life had been taken during a wrecking operation, the wrecker might be stoned to death. In some countries, England among them, the wrecker was chained to a post in his house and the house set afire.

Wreck of the packet ship *Albion* en route from London to New York. Of the 46 on board, only six survived (Mariners Museum, Newport News, Va.).

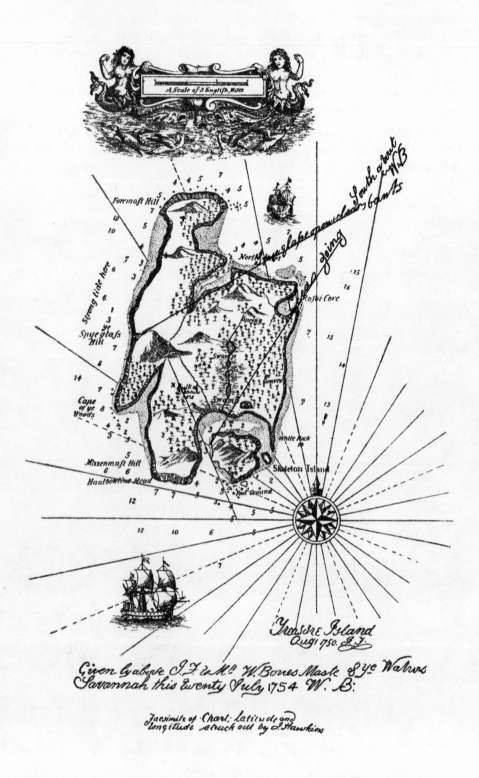

The treasure map drawn by Robert Louis Stevenson and his stepson. The map inspired Stevenson to write the story explaining it, *Treasure Island*.

Treasure Island

Piracy has proved to be a lavish source of inspiration for writers and storytellers of all kinds. Its stark and bloody histories and its exotic settings bearing the promise of unimagined riches are made to order for creative embellishment. This brief chapter will examine one instance of how the tapestry of legend and myth has been woven out of the strands of the actual details of the practice of piracy.

Pirates' careers were for the most part brief. The majority ended their days in obscurity or on the gallows. Those who survived often did so lacking all of the parts with which nature endowed them. Pirate codes go into specific detail about compensation for loss of limbs, eyes, etc. For the most part their service was uncomfortable, unhealthy, and tedious. And yet there were no doubt moments of high adventure in the life of the pirate. Piracy offered a unique measure of freedom, at a time when the common lot was one dictated by the rhythms and demands of agricultural economies, the unquestioning assumptions of a rigid class structure, and the stern dictates of scriptural morality. The cities offered more varied diversions than the country, but the urban poor for the most part had even less to look forward to. Only wealth and high position ensured a reasonably comfortable existence and the scope to pursue one's interests.

For those not so fortunate, the sea provided the most accessible means of escape as well as the promise of exciting new experiences. As we have seen, conditions in the navy and on merchant ships, however, ranged from rigorous to brutal. Ship captains were autocrats at sea, and often their rule was tyrannical. In fact, harsh treatment, particularly aboard merchant vessels, led many a seaman to turn to piracy. In comparison pirate society was constructed along egalitarian lines. Pirate codes, which were adopted by most companies, legislated that profits be shared equitably and that captains serve at the will of the majority.

These factors explain to some extent why pirates are so often depicted sympathetically in fiction. Of course the darker side of the pirate's career is not without its own appeal. The early influential "historical" accounts of pirates played up their cruelty, violence, and frequent use of torture. The reader of today's tabloids should not be surprised that such descriptions found a receptive audience.

Portrait of Robert Louis Stevenson by Sir William Blake Richmond (National Portrait Gallery, London).

In many respects the propagation of the legend of piracy has much in common with that of the American West. In both cases the relationship between the fact and the fictions it generated are complex and interesting. Pirates, like western heroes and outlaws, are first met with in childhood. This inevitably colors our perception of them. When it comes to pirates the adult still harbors some of Peter Pan's enthusiasm; they remain larger than life.

In addition, contemporary accounts of both pirates and western heroes and villains are unreliable and often contradictory, though it must be admitted that the chroniclers of the old West were more prone to wild exaggeration and aggrandizement. Finally, both recount adventures in worlds beyond the reckoning of civilization, where one might as easily encounter gallantry as bestiality.

There are, however, some important ways in which the development of the myth of piracy differs from that of the old West. Perhaps the most significant is that while the imaginary notion of life in the old West has been shaped by many quasi-historical accounts — tales of Billy the Kid, Jesse James, Wyatt Earp, etc. — the image conjured up by the mention of the word pirate is in large measure due to one work, whose entire cast of characters was the product of one man's imagination.

Robert Louis Stevenson was thirty-one years old when he began work on an adventure story he entitled *The Sea Cook*. The tale started with a map that he drew with his stepson, Lloyd Osbourne. Osbourne, who was twelve years old at the time, later recalled the events of that day:

> One rainy morning, busy with a box of paints, I happened to be tinting the map of an island that I had drawn. Stevenson came in as I was finishing it, and with his affectionate interest in everything I was doing, leaned over my shoulder, and was soon elaborating the map, and naming it. I shall never forget the thrill of Skeleton Island, Spy-Glass Hill, or the heart stirring climax of the three red crosses. And the greater climax still when he wrote down the words "Treasure Island" at the top right hand corner.

The map took root in Stevenson's imagination and turned out to be the catalyst for the creation of a classic. Up until this point he had been a struggling writer whose work had met with a lukewarm reception. Through good fortune his fledgling manuscript came to the attention of the publisher of a magazine for boys, called *Young Folks*. Stevenson entered into a contract to bring it out in serial form.

The first chapters rolled out with ease. But after transporting the cast to Treasure Island and setting them at each other's throats, his inspiration faltered. Stevenson recounted his state of mind at that juncture.

Long John Silver leading the captive Jim Hawkins. N.C. Wyeth illustration for *Treasure Island*.

Old Blind Pew deserted by his companions. N.C. Wyeth illustration for *Treasure Island*.

I was thirty-one; I was the head of a family; I had lost my health; I had never paid my way, had never yet made over £200 a year ... I was indeed close on despair.

Over the following winter he moved the family to Switzerland and there regained his stride. "I sat down one morning to write," he said, "and behold! it flowed from me like small talk." He had soon completed the story that would make him famous and secure for him a permanent place in the pantheon of English writers.

Stevenson's achievement in *Treasure Island* is a multi-levelled one. His narrative is straightforward and compelling. He chooses a young boy, Jim Hawkins, as his primary narrator. Hawkins is intelligent and resourceful, but also sufficiently credulous to take the pirates at their own estimation. At the center of the story is the one-legged pirate, turned sea cook, Long John Silver. Buoyant, sardonic, and altogether memorable, Silver's character vividly comes to life. Though he is cunning and duplicitous, his humor and vitality ultimately win over the reader's sympathies. Despite his double-dealing, he is a companion that we could all wish for. In this portrait Stevenson definitively embodies the ambivalent nature of the response to piracy that can, as we have seen, be found as far back as Thucydides. While pirates have been condemned, hunted down, and extirpated, their free and easy lives of adventure have provoked envy and admiration. In this way *Treasure Island* has become the summation of a whole range of attitudes towards piracy.

From its first scenes the uncanny, marvelous world of dark fears, intoxication, violence, and the lure of treasure break in on the ordinary life of a young boy. With the arrival of Billy Bones and the haunting visit of Blind Pew, immediately, almost effortlessly, the narrative is set into motion. There is no need to retell such a well-known story, but the reader with even a passing knowledge of pirate lore will delight in the numerous references to the trade that Stevenson slyly inserts. The ship Jim and his party set sail on is named the *Hispaniola*, the main Caribbean stopover for Spanish gold on its way back to Europe. And if Jim Hawkins, for instance, had known more he certainly would have become suspicious as Silver lists the piratical bona fides of his parrot, whose only words were "pieces of eight":

"Now that bird," [Silver] would say, "is, may be, two hundred years old, Hawkins — they lives forever mostly; and if anybody's seen more wickedness, it must be the devil himself. She's sailed with England, the great Cap'n England, the pirate. She's been at Madagascar, and at Malabar, and Surinam, and Providence and Portobello. She was at the fishing up of the wrecked Plate ships. It's

Hawkins in the treasure cave, where X marked the spot. N.C. Wyeth
illustration for *Treasure Island*.

there she learned 'Pieces of eight,' and little wonder; three hundred and fifty thousand of 'em, Hawkins! She was at the boarding of the Viceroy of the Indies out of Goa, she was . . ."

Clearly an indisputable piratical pedigree!

A little later on Hawkins overhears a conversation that finally alerts him to Silver's true calling.

"It was a master surgeon, him that ampytated me . . . but he was hanged like a dog, and sun-dried like the rest, at Corso Castle. That was Roberts' men [Bartholomew Roberts], that was, and comed of changing names o their ships — Royal Fortune and so on. Now what a ship was christened, so let her stay, I says. So it was with the Cassandra, as brought us all safe home from Malabar, after England took the Viceroy of the Indies."

Silver continues:

"Here it is about gentlemen of fortune. They lives rough, and they risk swinging, but they eat and drink like fighting cocks, and when a cruise is done, why it's hundreds of pounds instead of hundreds of farthings in their pockets. Now the most goes for rum and a good fling, and to sea again in their shirts . . ."

The buried treasure that lies at the heart of the narrative has become an accepted feature of pirate lore. Stevenson fostered the impression that the entire Caribbean is dotted with graves filled with gold and jewels. But the reader may want to pause before taking up pick and shovel. Pirates almost never buried their plunder. Stevenson probably got the idea from rumors that circulated about Captain Kidd. Kidd did a lot of business with merchants in New York. Facing the threat of capture, he evidently buried some of his gains on Gardiners Island off the east coast of Long Island. Although the exact amount is in dispute, one of the Gardiners agreed to pay a certain sum as compensation. But Kidd was the exception. Pirates as a rule were notorious for spending whatever they had as soon as they had it.

The successful creation of a fictional world depends on the authority of the writer's voice. Author and authority are closely related words. Stevenson was experienced at sea having sailed on a schooner. The *Hispaniola* was created in its image. His knowledge of the sea and sailing are seen throughout, as when the captain remarks of the *Hispaniola*: "She'll lie a point nearer to the wind than a man has a right to expect of his own married wife, sir." But when describing the process by which he came to write *Treasure Island*, Stevenson returns to the importance of a map, and not only because it prevents him from making obvious mistakes:

> The author must know his countryside whether real or imaginary, like his hand . . . . It is my contention — my superstition, if you like — that he who is faithful to his map, and consults it, and draws from it his inspiration, daily and hourly, gains positive support, and not mere negative immunity from accident. The tale has root there; it grows in that soil; it has a spine of its own behind the words.

OVERLEAF — Dead Men Tell No Tales. Howard Pyle.

A Brief Glossary
of Piratical Terms

ACCOUNT, TO GO ON THE: to embark on a piratical cruise

ACTS OF PARDON OR GRACE: general amnesty under which a reformed pirate might surrender in return for a certificate of pardon

BALLAST: heavy material used to stabilize a vessel, especially one not carrying cargo

BARKADEER: a small pier or jetty

BARQUE: a sailing ship of three or more masts having the foremasts rigged square and the aftermast rigged for fore and aft

BILGED ON HER ANCHOR: a ship holed or pierced by its own anchor

BOOMS OR FENDERS: spars to which a sail is fastened to control its position relative to the wind

BOOT-TOPPING: a hurried, partial careen

BOWSPRIT: a spar projecting from the bow of a vessel used to carry the headstay as far forward as possible

BRIG, BRIGANTINE: a two-masted sailing ship, rigged square on the foremast and fore and aft with square topsails on the mainmast

'BROUGHT A SPRING UPON HER CABLE': came round in a different direction

BRULOT (FRENCH): a fireship

BUCCANEERS: the original "cow killers" who settled illegally on Hispaniola. The name derives from their method of smoke-curing meat on a boucan. Later, in the seventeenth and eighteenth centuries, they took to sea and preyed on Spanish colonies and shipping in America and the Caribbean.

CAPSTAN: a windlass with a vertical drum, used for hauling in ropes, etc.

CAREEN: to cause a vessel to keel over on its side in order to clean or repair its bottom

CAREENAGE: a careening place

CHASE GUNS: cannon situated at the bow of a ship, used during pursuit

CHEQUEEN: sequin, a former Venetian gold coin

CLAP IN IRONS: to chain

CRIMP: a person who swindled or press ganged sailors

DORY: a fisherman's dugout

DOUBLOON: a former Spanish gold coin

DROGER: a West Indian coasting vessel

EXECUTION DOCK: the usual place for pirate hangings, on the Thames, in London near the Tower

FIRESHIP: a vessel loaded with explosives and used as a bomb by igniting it and directing it to drift among an enemy's warships

FLOTILLA: a small fleet

FLYING JIB: the jib furthest forward on a vessel with two or more jibs

FREEBOOTER OR FILIBUSTER: another name for a buccaneer or pirate

GALLEON: a large sailing ship having three or more masts, lateen-rigged on the aftermasts and square-rigged on the fore and mainmasts; used as a warship or for trade

GALLEY: a low, flat-built vessel, propelled partly or wholly by oars

GIBBET: a wooden structure resembling a gallows from which bodies of executed criminals were hung for public view

GRAPPLE OR GRAPNEL: a hooked instrument thrown with a rope for gripping and closing with an enemy

GRENADE: these were made from square-faced case bottles, filled with gunpowder, small shot, bits of old iron, and thrown by hand

GUARDA COSTA: a vessel fitted out in Spanish or colonial ports and commissioned by local governors to enforce Spain's trade monopoly

GUINEAMAN: a ship engaged in the slave trade in the Guinea Coast of West Africa

HEAVE DOWN, TO: to turn a vessel on its side for cleaning

HOGSHEAD: a large cask used mainly for shipment of wines and spirits

INTERLOPER: an illegal trader

JACK: a flag, especially one flown at the bow of a ship to indicate her nationality

JOLLY ROGER: the pirate flag

LARBOARD: the left (or port) side of a vessel when facing the bow

LETTERS OF MARQUE OR REPRISAL: commissions or licenses to fit out armed vessels to be employed in the capture of enemy merchant shipping and to commit other hostile acts that would otherwise be condemned as piracy

MAINSHEET: the line used to control the angle of the mainsail to the wind

MAN-OF-WAR: a warship

MAROON, TO: to put ashore and abandon a person on a barren island or cay

MAROONERS: a name sometimes given to pirates because of their use of marooning as a form of punishment

MOIDORE: a former Portuguese gold coin

PATARERO: a kind of muzzle-loading mortar that fired scattering shot, stones, spikes, old nails, broken glass, etc.

PIECE OF EIGHT: a former Spanish coin

PINNACE: any of various kinds of ship's tender

PIRAGUA: a type of native dugout canoe

PRESS (OR FORCE): to recruit for naval or military service by forcible means

PRIVATEER: a privately owned, armed vessel operating under letters of marque

QUARTER: mercy shown to a defeated opponent. Also a ship's quarter is that part of a vessel's side towards the stern, usually aft of the aftermost mast.

ROAD: a partly sheltered anchorage

SALMAGUNDI: a dish of chopped meat, eggs, anchovies, onions, etc.; a pirate favorite

SCHOONER: a sailing vessel with at least two masts with all lower sails rigged fore and aft

SEA ARTIST: sailing master

SLOOP: a single-masted vessel rigged fore and aft with a long bowsprit, much favored by the pirates because of its shallow draught and maneuverability

SMACK: a sailing vessel usually sloop-rigged, used in coasting or fishing

SNOW: a small sailing vessel, resembling a brig, carrying a main and foremast and a supplementary trysail mast close behind the mainmast

SPANISH MAIN: the mainland of Spanish America, from the Isthmus of Panama to the present republics of Colombia and Venezuela

SPIKE (GUNS): to render a gun useless by blocking the vent or touch hole with a spike, often a soft nail

SPRITSAIL YARD: a yard set on the underside of the bowsprit, to carry a spritsail

STARBOARD: the right side of a vessel when facing the bow

STRIKE (COLORS): to haul down a ship's flag as a signal of surrender

SWEET TRADE: buccaneering or piracy

SWIVEL (GUN): a gun mounted on a pivot so that it might be swung from side to side

TENDER: a small boat, towed or carried by a ship

VICE-ADMIRALTY COURTS: courts established in the British colonies for trial and decision of maritime questions and offenses

WALK THE PLANK: a method of disposing of prisoners at sea; popular belief to the contrary it was not a usual practice among pirates

WARP: to move a vessel by hauling on a rope fixed to a stationary object ashore

WEIGH: to raise a vessel's anchor in preparation for departure

WHERRY: a light rowing boat, used in inland waters and harbors

YARDS: the spars slung from the masts of a square-rigged vessel and used for suspending sails